National Urban League
Negro membership
in American labor unions

LENDING POLICY

IF YOU DAMAGE OR LOSE LIBRARY
MATERIALS, THEN YOU WILL BE
CHARGED FOR REPLACEMENT. FAIL-
URE TO PAY AFFECTS LIBRARY
PRIVILEGES, GRADES, TRANSCRIPTS,
DIPLOMAS, AND REGISTRATION
PRIVILEGES OR ANY COMBINATION
THEREOF.

NEGRO MEMBERSHIP IN AMERICAN LABOR UNIONS

by

THE DEPARTMENT OF RESEARCH AND INVESTIGATIONS

of

THE NATIONAL URBAN LEAGUE

IRA DE A. REID, *Director*

NEGRO UNIVERSITIES PRESS
NEW YORK

Originally published in 1930
by the Alexander Press

Reprinted 1969 by
Negro Universities Press
A DIVISION OF GREENWOOD PUBLISHING CORP.
NEW YORK

SBN 8371-1923-5

I

"Nope, I won't scab, but I ain't a joiner kind of fellah," said Jake. "I ain't no white folk's nigger, and I ain't no poor white's fool. When I longshored in Philly I was a good union man. But when I made New York I done finds out that they gives the colored mens the worser piers and holds the best o' them job for the Irishmen. No, pardner keep you' card. I take the best I kin get as I goes mah way. But I tell you, things ain't at all lovely between white and black in this heah Gawd's own country."

II

"But it ain't decent to scab,' said Jake.—

"Decent mah black moon!" shouted Zeddy, I'll scab through hell to make mah living. Scab job or open shop or union am all the same jobs to me. White mens don't want niggers in them unions nohow. Ain't you a good carpenter? And ain't I a good blacksmith? But kain we get a lookin on our trade heah in this white man's city? Ain't white mens done scabbed niggers outa all the jobs they useter hold down heah in this city? Waiter, bootblack, and barber shop?—I got to live and I'll scab through hell to live."

"Home to Harlem"

CLAUDE McKAY.

CONTENTS

NEGRO MEMBERSHIP IN AMERICAN LABOR UNIONS

LIST OF TABLES

PREFACE

This study of Negro membership in labor unions was prompted by the almost utter absence of any recent authentic and comprehensive information about the matter. *The Atlanta University Studies* of 1902 and 1912, and Wolfe's *Admission to American Trade Unions,* 1911 were the latest studies on the extent of labor organization among Negro workers. Wesley's *History of Negro Labor in the United States* (1927) outlined the attitude of organized labor, and traced the organizing efforts of various unions. In addition to these works, there were a few local studies and numerous magazine articles, none of which, however, covered the whole field of Negro membership.

Any research group attempting such a study as this is at the mercy of several handicaps, not the least of which is the absence of any central body of data or records. At the same time, where relations between white and black unionists are most friendly the items of particular race or specific color have been disregarded, the workers being merged under one classification—Americans. This policy, itself, which is the ultimate objective of those who insist upon the full inclusion of Negroes in labor unions made excessively difficult the gauging of the present numerical volume of this Negro inclusion.

Negro Membership in American Labor Unions was made possible by a grant from the American Fund for Public Service in 1925. The study was initiated by Charles S. Johnson, Director of Research for the National Urban League at that time. Under his supervision, the major portion of the field work and distribution of questionnaires was done. A preliminary report on the progress of the study was made in 1926. It was not until 1928 that sufficient information was available to permit a more exhaustive treatment of the subject. Because the changes in materials of this sort are gross and constant, it was necessary that Ira De A. Reid, who succeeded Mr. Johnson as Director of Research in 1928, recheck much of the information already received and conclude the investigations. The completion of these processes enabled the preparation of the report.

The facts set forth in this study should enable one to obtain a fair estimate of the status of the Negro worker in the American Labor movement. No effort has been herein made to present a critical analysis of the factors underlying his position, rather is the purpose to present a picture of the method by which Negro workers have entered labor unions, the exclusion policies of national bodies, the types of union membership, the extent to which Negro workers are organized, and their experiences within and without the union.

Grateful acknowledgments are made to those many persons within and without the labor movement whose materials, suggestions and criticisms have been invaluable aids in the development of this project.

I. De A. R.

New York, New York.
January, 1930.

THE INDUSTRIAL STATUS OF THE NEGRO

That the problems of Negro workers and organized labor may be seen more clearly the industrial status of the Negro group must be considered. What are Negro workers doing? How is their labor utilized? Do the "Negro jobs" of the century's early years continue? Have Negroes broken through the economic and industrial deadlines established against them?

The terrific pressure exerted by slavery upon the white laboring classes was being released in the latter years of the 19th century. Jobs formerly classified as "Negro jobs", and which no white man would accept, were filled by white workers. The depletion of the soil in agricultural communities and the disappearance of free land, were causing Negroes to desert the farms of the South for newer fields in the midwest in the first instance, and to seek urban communities in the second. The increased competition between the two racial groups led to the exclusion of the minority group in practically all occupational lines except domestic service.

In the North the newer immigrants were usurping the unskilled industrial positions, while the Germans, English, Irish, Swedes and Greeks were making severe inroads upon the traditional occupations as domestics, caterers, bootblacks, butlers and coachmen. Thus appeared a racial stratification of American labor that was rapidly relegating the Negro to a most insignificant status in all occupational groupings other than agriculture and domestic service.

Between 1900 and 1910 there was an era of advancement in the skilled trades. The Negro population in 1900 found its greatest occupational importance in agriculture, and in domestic and personal service. The native whites were most extensively employed in agriculture, manufacturing and in the mechanical pursuits; the foreign born whites found their greatest importance in the manufacturing and mechanical pursuits and in personal and domestic service. Among Negroes, agricultural occupations increased 35 per cent, trade and transportation increased 103 per cent, domestic and personal serviced increase 17 per cent, while the jobs in which Negroes were engaged in the manufacturing and mechanical pursuits increased 156 per cent. In 1900 the number of Negro workers in factories was 131,216 but the number increased to 358.180 or 173 per cent in 1910. The textile industries employed eight thousand more Negroes in unskilled positions in 1910 than in 1900, the number increasing from 2,949 to 11,333, or 283 per cent.

During the period prior to the World War the repeated efforts of Negro spokesmen and interested white persons to entrench Negro workers in industrial positions, with such increments as might accrue to them from these positions, were futile. For one hundred years, America had relied almost entirely upon the European immigrants who had come to their shores for its industrial labor and the adjustment of this immigrant group was considered more satisfactory than could be expected of the Negro worker. The World War, however, exerted profound changes. This immigration was suddenly checked. New recruits for industry were necessary and the Negro was the most available supply. The activities of labor agents were bringing Negro workers into northern industries in great numbers. They went into those industries needing masses of unskilled workers—the steel and iron industries, construction, stockyards, railroads, road maintenance and construction. In many instances they entered as strike-breakers. These new industrial opportunities were in no small way responsible for the migration of 1,200,000 Negroes who moved from South to North between 1915 and 1928.

The results of this mass movement have been intricate and manifold. For the first time the economic and industrial status of the Negro has received attention as an integral element in the problems of the relationship of worker and industry. As early as 1923 the U. S. Department of Labor reported an increase of employment in skilled lines of 34 per cent. Some states showed increases as high as 186 per cent. Steel and iron workers in Pittsburgh increased from less than 100 in five plants in 1910 to 16,900 in 23 plants in 1923. In August of that year the Carnegie Steel Company alone employed 6,758 Negro workers. The Ford plant in Detroit employed 11,000 Negro workers. Chicago showed great gains in iron and steel as well as in the packing industries. Meanwhile physical conflicts resulted. White workers threatened to quit work if Negroes were employed. Many did. Southern whites were imported to northern mills as foremen. Trade unions sought Negro members. Negroes remained skeptical. The period was fraught with so many difficulties that each new day brought new analyses and new conclusions regarding the efficiency of that labor. One group of employment managers in Pittsburgh classified races on the basis of their efficiency in certain types of industrial activity. In this scale the Negro ranked nineteenth among thirty-seven races and nationalities. Interesting, however, was the conviction in one plant that Negroes are excellent workers on operations of severe heat. In this plant they were employed in the heat of the open hearth furnaces dur-

TABLE I

Number and Per Cent Distribution of Negro Persons 10 Years of Age and Over Engaged in Each General Division of Occupations for the United States. 1920-1910

1920

	BOTH SEXES		MALE		FEMALE	
	Number	Per Cent	Number	Per Cent	Number	Per Cent
ALL OCCUPATIONS	4,824,151	11.6	3,252,862	9.8	1,571,289	18.4
Agriculture, Forestry and Animal Husbandry	2,178,888	19.9	1,566,627	15.9	612,261	56.5
Extraction of Minerals	73,229	6.7	72,892	6.7	337	11.8
Manufacturing and Mechanical Industries	886,810	6.9	781,827	7.2	104,983	5.4
Transportation	312,421	10.2	308,896	10.8	3,525	1.7
Trade	140,467	3.3	129,309	3.6	11,158	1.7
Public Service	50,552	6.6	49,586	6.6	966	4.4
Professional Service	80,183	3.7	41,056	3.6	39,127	3.8
Domestic and Personal Service	1,065,590	31.3	273,959	22.5	790,631	36.2
Clerical Occupations	37,001	1.2	28,710	1.7	8,301	0.6

1910

	BOTH SEXES		MALE		FEMALE	
	Number	Per Cent	Number	Per Cent	Number	Per Cent
ALL OCCUPATIONS	5,192,535	13.6	3,178,554	10.6	2,013,981	24.9
Agriculture, Forestry and Animal Husbandry	2,893,375	22.9	1,842,238	17.0	1,051,137	58.2
Extraction of Minerals	61,129	6.3	61,048	6.3	81	7.4
Manufacturing and Mechanical Industries	631,280	5.9	563,343	6.4	67,937	3.7
Transportation	255,945	9.7	254,659	10.1	1,286	1.2
Trade	119,491	3.3	112,464	3.6	7,027	1.5
Public Service	22,382	4.9	22,033	4.9	349	2.6
Professional Service	67,335	4.0	37,690	3.9	29,645	4.0
Domestic and Personal Service	1,222,262	29.7	268,875	21.7	853,387	33.7
Clerical Occupations	19,336	1.1	16,204	1.4	3,132	0.5

ing the summer months, and were assigned to outside duties in the winter.

The present distribution of Negro workers cannot be told completely, though the 1920 census findings are indicative of trends. The 11,650,000 Negroes in the United States representing 9.9 per cent of the population do approximately 12 per cent of all the work. If, however, his opportunity for employment were equal to that of other racial groups there would be many changes in the occupational distribution. On the basis of the amount of work to be done, the Negro is overemployed in agriculture and domestic service, and underemployed in the other occupational classes. Moreover, the amount of underemployment among Negroes increased in Trade, Public Service, Professional Service and Clerical Work between 1910 and 1920. Despite the fact that there have been losses in the number of gainfully employed persons in both agricultural and domestic occupations, one finds that on the basis of total man power used in these various groupings, the Negro has lost ground while the total trend has been toward increases in the number of employed.

TABLE II

Per Cent of Underemployment and Overemployment of Negro Workers in Major Occupational Groupings 1910 and 1920 and Per Cent of Change in These Groupings

OCCUPATIONAL GROUPINGS	1910 Per Cent		1920 Per Cent		1910 - 1920 Per Cent Change	
	Over-Employment	Under-Employment	Over-Employment	Under-Employment	Over-Employment	Under-Employment
Agriculture	22.5		18.9		3.6	
Extraction of Minerals		1.3		1.1		—0.2
Manufacturing and Mechanical Industries		15.6		12.4		—3.2
Transportation		2.0		0.9		—1.1
Trade		7.3		7.2		—0.1
Public Service		0.9		0.9		—0.1
Professional Service		3.1		3.5		+0.4
Domestic and Personal Service	11.7		13.9		+2.2	
Clerical Workers		4.2		6.7		—2.5

TABLE III

Gains and Losses in Per Cent of Population Ten Years of Age and Over and Gainfully Employed Population by Sex and Classes of Population—1910-1920

POPULATION GROUP	Per Cent Change in Total Population in 10 years of Age and Over	MALE		FEMALE		
		Per Cent Change in Gainfully Employed Population	Per Cent Change in Total Population	Per Cent Change in Gainfully Employed Population	Per Cent Change in Total Population	Per Cent Change in Gainfully Employed Population
Native White, Native Parentage	+1.5	+2.3	+1.8	+1.4	+1.2	+5.3
Native White, Foreign or Mixed Parentage	+0.8	+1.7	+1.9	+1.3	+0.7	+3.4
Foreign Born White	−1.8	−1.9	−2.3	−1.9	−1.3	−2.0
Negro	−1.5	−2.0	−0.3	−0.8	−0.7	−6.5
Other	−0.1	−0.1	−0.1	−0.1	−0.0	−0.0

In explanation of the foregoing table it should be noted that though Negroes formed 1.5 per cent less of the total population ten years of age and over in 1920 than in 1910, they did 2 per cent less of the work; that the male population was 0.3 per cent less but did 0.8 per cent less of the work; that the female population was 0.7 per cent less but did 6.5 per cent less of the work done by women. The decrease in agricultural employment will not in itself account for these losses.

A further analysis of the census material reveals interesting information regarding the occupational distribution of Negro workers. The Negro provides 75 per cent of the fertilizer laborers, 33 per cent of the tobacco workers, 14 per cent of the iron and steel laborers, 33 per cent of the laborers in lumber and furniture industries and 20 per cent of the helpers in the building and hand trades. He also provides 42 per cent of the fish packing and curing hands. 29 per cent of the glass workers, 32 per cent of the longshoremen and 28 per cent of the railroad laborers. Between 1910 and 1920 semi-skilled Negro workers in slaughtering and packing houses increased 1,832 per cent, laborers in iron and steel increased 237 per cent, while laborers in food industries increased 261 per cent. Meanwhile, the number of Negroes in the following occupations decreased from 24 to 100 per cent—captains, masters and pilots of vessels, motormen, freight agents, express agents, steam railway conductors, telephone and telegraph linesmen, firemen in fire departments, mechanical engineers, waiters, bell boys, butlers and several others. Selected occupations in which the Negro formed 10 per cent or more of the total workers in 1920 are presented in the table on following pages.

There is a marked tendency in the American occupational scheme toward job usurpation for the American whites of native parentage and those of foreign and mixed parentage. Between 1910 and 1920 the foreign born worker as well as the Negro worker showed losses in their ratio to the total gainfully employed population at an acceleration in excess of their relation to the total population ten years of age and over.

The industrial employment of Negro women prior to 1928 was negligible. The Federal census of 1920 showed that they constituted from one-fourth to one-third of those women reported working in the manufacture of wood products, hosiery, tobacco, bags, and waste and glass. They formed from 28 to 52 per cent of those working in three different food industries. Between 1910 and 1920 the proportion of Negro women in manufacturing and mechanical industries nearly doubled, presenting a striking contrast to the employment of all women in those lines, which was comparatively slight.

The following analysis will indicate more clearly the advance made by the Negro woman worker: In 1910 of every 100 employed Negro women, approximately 50 were in agriculture, 40 were in domestic and personal service, and 10 were following other lines of work; but in 1920, of every 100 Negro women approximately 35 were in agriculture, 50 were in domestic and personal service and 15 were in other work. The largest numbers of those 15 were in tobacco, food products, textiles, and wood industries.

In the more or less skilled trades Negroes have a much smaller percentage of the total. In the United States there are only 56,000 Negro skilled craftsmen as compared with 1,371,000 pursuing unskilled occupations or employed as day laborers. These workers form 3.8 per cent of all carpenters, 5.5 per cent of iron molders, 1.2 per cent of all cotton mill workers and 3 per cent of the workers in oil and petroleum. Little hope for a greater inclusion in the building and hand trades is seen in the fact that Negroes form only 1.7 per cent of all apprentices in the building and hand trades.

Opportunities for apprenticeship training in special trades have shown greater restrictions than the trades themselves. The ten year period 1910-1920 added only 98 Negro apprentices while the total number of apprentices increased from 118.964 to 144,177. Blacksmiths, carpenters, brick masons and painters, for example, had fewer Negro apprentices in 1920 than in 1910 or 1900.

	1890	1900	1910	1920
Blacksmiths' Apprentices	226	131	178	161
Carpenters' Apprentices	263	123	253	198
Painters' Apprentices	51	85	68	80
Brick Masons' Apprentices	113	83	171	127

The number of workers in other trades shows similar variations.

TABLE IV

Occupational Distribution of Negro Workers in Selected Occupations Where They Form 10 Per Cent or More of the Total Workers Employed in 1920 and Distribution in these Occupations in 1920

OCCUPATION	1920			1910		
	TOTAL WORKERS	NEGRO WORKERS	PER CENT NEGRO	TOTAL WORKERS	NEGRO WORKERS	PER CENT NEGRO
AGRICULTURE						
Farm Laborers	1,850,119	653,217	35.3	3,310,534	1,145,353	34.6
Farm Laborers, working out	2,055,276	521,551	25.4	2,636,966	780,035	29.5
EXTRACTION OF MINERALS						
Quarry Operatives	45,162	6,326	14.0	80,480	9,953	12.3
MANUFACTURING AND MECHANICAL INDUSTRIES						
Firemen, Stationary	143,875	23,153	16.0	112,248	14,927	12.7
Laborers						
Fertilizer Factories	12,493	9,407	75.3	9,847	6,934	70.4
Cigar and Tobacco Factories	35,157	21,334	60.7	16,392	8,173	49.5
Clay, Glass and Slate Industries	124,544	18,753	15.5	154,826	22,523	14.5
Food Industries	59,548	27,730	17.4	33,903	7,670	22.6
Helpers, Building and Hand Trades	63,159	13,223	20.8	65,431	14,891	22.8
Iron and Steel Industries	729,613	105,641	14.4	482,941	31,307	*
Lumber and Furniture	320,613	100,276	33.1	317,244	98,054	30.6
Plasterers and Cement Finishers	45,876	7,082	15.4	47,682	6,175	12.9
Laborers, Building and not specified	623,203	134,828	21.6	869,478	157,657	18.1

SEMI-SKILLED OPERATIVES		7,544	15.1	25,897	391	*
Slaughter and Packing Houses	49,991					
Saw and Planing Mills	57,320					
Cigar and Tobacco Factories	145,222					
TRANSPORTATION						
Longshoremen, Stevedores	85,928	27,337	31.8	62,857	16,405	26.1
Sailors, Deck-hands	54,832	7,232	13.0	46,510	6,508	14.0
Chauffeurs	285,045	38,573	13.5	45,785	4,676	11.2
Draymen, Teamsters	411,132	56,714	13.8	408,469	50,711	12.4
Laborers, Steam Railroad	470,199	97,979	28.4	543,168	87,188	16.7
Laborers, Street Railroad	25,514	4,164	16.3	27,807	3,372	12.1
TRADE						
Deliverymen, stores	149,347	24,398	16.3	205,589	119,491	15.1
Laborers, Coal, Lumber Yards	125,609	27,497	21.9	81,123	12,772	15.6
Laborers, Porters in Stores	125,007	40,885	32.6	102,333	37,576	36.7
PROFESSIONAL SERVICE						
Clergymen	127,270	19,571	15.4	118,018	17,495	14.8
DOMESTIC AND PERSONAL SERVICE						
Bootblacks	15,175	5,660	36.7	14,020	3,850	27.4
Elevator Tenders	40,713	10,334	25.6	25,035	6,278	25.0
Waiters and Waitresses	228,985	45,836	20.0	188,293	43,078	22.9
Charwomen, Cleaners	36,803	9,283	25.2	34,034	8,559	25.1
Laundresses (not in laundry)	396,756	288,763	72.7	533,697	368,124	69.0
Bell Boys	17,231	6,929	40.2	18,329	8,212	44.8
Chambermaids	29,302	10,453	35.6	39,789	14,082	35.4
Cooks	398,475	202,435	50.8	450,440	238,392	52.9
Janitors, Sextons	178,628	44,128	24.1	113,081	27,171	24.6
Porters, Steam R. R.	22,513	20,224	90.0	17,298	15,116	87.4
Porters (except in stores)	65,655	39,207	59.6	67,830	37,442	55.2

[15]

* Less than 10 Per Cent.

TABLE V
Negroes in Selected Occupations of the Building and Hand Trades—1890-1920

	1890	1900	1910	1920
Bricklayers and Masons..	9,467	14,387	12,016	10.609
Carpenters	22,318	21,114	29,043	34,243
Plasterers	4,006	3.757	6,175	8,034
Painters	4,396	5,784	8,040	7,082
Paper Hangers	274	586	968	954
Plumbers	616	1,193	1,996	3.516
Roofers	243	368	613	609
Electricians			96	1,342

The economic status of the Negro as well as his opportunity of employment varies with the sections of the country. While the North is beginning to give Negroes opportunity in major industrial fields, the development of skill in the hand crafts and various other occupations has taken place in the South. In Georgia, for example, are found more locomotive firemen than in all the northern states combined. New York provides more jobs for male workers in domestic and personal service. South Carolina, Alabama and Georgia in 1920 employed more than half of the colored painters and paper hangers in the country, while Pennsylvania accounted for one-tenth of all the Negro chauffeurs.

Wages received by Negro workers are, in the main, lower than that of the white workers, even for the same type of work. Current explanations for this difference in earnings are many. Chief among them is the statement that the Negro workers' standard of living is lower than that of the white worker. As a result the wages of Negroes reach a subsistence level. They have been able to live on less than the white worker because they have been compelled to do so. It has become necessary for the Negro to be an opportunist in the matter of wages. "Working in an industrial plant on the same operations with white workers, as skilled or unskilled operatives, they get the same wages as others —working exclusively as a racial group in a department of a business, as, for instance, an all-Negro force of janitors, stock-girls, messengers, shipping clerks, their pay is apt to be less than that received by whites. Working as the only wage earners of a business such as building tradesmen, laundresses, garment workers, the rule is to force upon them smaller compensation than white would get—an arrangement assuring Negroes employment they otherwise would not have and employers a savings in wages. Union membership does not always remove the lower wage, for unions sometimes permit a double standard."[1]

[1] Vide: Hill, T. Arnold. Negro Labor—American Federationist— Volume 35, No. 12—December, 1928.

The most complete data on variations between the wages of white and Negro workers are found in the reports of the Commissioner of Labor of Virginia. A summary of the 1927 report shows that the average daily wages varied as follows:

	WHITE	COLORED
Apprentices	$3.35	$3.00
Bricklayers	11.00	9.60
Carpenters	6.24	4.22
Cement Workers	6.33	4.42
Electricians	6.36	....
Engineers	7.87	....
Helpers	3.37	3.08
Laborers	3.25	3.06
Lathers	6.08	5.40
Painters and Decorators	5.81	4.00
Plasterers	9.26	9.12
Plumbers and Gasfitters	4.49	4.04
Sheet Metal Workers	6.16	4.75
Slaters and Tile Setters	8.37	....
Steam Fitters	9.33	....
Miscellaneous	4.29	2.75

The Bureau of Labor Statistics made a study of wages and hours in cotton compresses in 1927. This study covered the states of Alabama, Arkansas, Georgia, Louisiana, Mississippi, North Carolina, Oklahoma, South Carolina. Tennessee and Texas. In 67 establishment covering 4,071 male and 106 female workers of whom 2,873 males were Negroes as were all of the females, the investigation reported as follows on the average earnings:

ALL STATES	PER HOUR AVERAGE EARNINGS	PER WEEK FULL TIME
MARKERS		
White	$0.400	$24.00
Colored	0.284	16.16
WEIGHERS AND CHECKERS		
White	0.479	29.24
Colored	0.275	14.95
OPENERS (dinkey press)		
White	0.250	15.00
Colored	0.300	17.43
TRUCKERS		
White	2.76	16.56
Colored	2.64	14.84
SAMPLERS		
White	0.464	27.84
Colored	0.328	18.83

In no one of the ten states were the earnings of Negro workers as much as that of the white workers, while Alabama and South Carolina showed actual earnings of Negroes to be less than one-half that of white workers. In Texas where Mexican workers were used, earnings per week for whites were $26.97, Negroes $20.15, Mexicans $17.37.

The studies of women workers in southern states made by the Women's Bureau in every instance show the wages of Negro women to be lower than that received by the white women workers.

Though the unusual demand for Negro labor has disappeared, it appears certain that this group has become a permanent factor in American industry. An analysis has been made of this situation by the Federal Department of Labor.[1] Representatives of this office studied the payrolls of 273 employers of Negro labor during the year prior to April 30, 1923 in California, Connecticut, Delaware, Illinois, Indiana, Kansas, Kentucky, Maryland, Massachusetts, Michigan, Missouri, New Jersey, New York, Oklahoma, Ohio and Wisconsin. The industries included machinery, tobacco, iron and steel, food stuffs, brass, brick, rubber, railroad equipment, and occupations in the fields of transportation, construction and railroad work. Negro workers during that period increased by 18,050. Of this number 13,893 were unskilled and 4,157 skilled. The skilled workers increased 38.5 per cent an the unskilled increased 44.0 per cent. The following table gives the increase for both groups.[2]

TABLE VI
Increase of Skilled and Unskilled Negro Workers in Selected Industries of 14 States—April, 1922 - April, 1923

STATES	INCREASE PER CENT	SKILLED PER CENT	UNSKILLED PER CENT
Maryland	55.48	186.86	27.67
Connecticut	88.74	90.48	88.58
Michigan	66.77	70.73	62.48
Kansas	40.42	68.97	37.13
Ohio	69.93	68.04	71.21
California	66.67	60.00	68.00
Pennsylvania	64.91	43.68	77.52
Illinois	45.14	39.94	46.69
Wisconsin	58.24	33.33	60.48
New York	37.19	30.00	37.79
Indiana	70.17	18.18	102.86
Kentucky	24.00	13.93	27.15
New Jersey	74.82	12.96	85.15
Oklahoma	14.10	3.85	15.67

[1] The Department of Labor, Office of the Secretary. Release, July 19, 1923.
[2] See Wesley, Charles H., Negro Labor in the United States, p. 300.

There has always existed a body of beliefs regarding the efficiency of Negro labor. It has been called wasteful—inefficient, lazy and indifferent. Negro workers are said to be an asset only when working in gangs under white supervision. The most complete analysis however is that formerly used as the basis for the employment of Negro workers in a large industrial center. In these industries the Negro worker was classified "*good*" in the following capacities,—with the pick and shovel, in carrying material as lumber and steel, at repairing roads, at building and demolition, at work requiring speed, on hot and dry operations, on wet and hot operations, where there are fumes and smoke, on oily work and on shifts. He was "*fair*" in concrete, with the wheelbarrow, as a hod carrier, in cleaning tracks, as a trucker, in repairing tracks, at shoveling material in bulk, at coal pushing and as a fireman, on stills and furnaces. as a rigger's helper, as a boilermaker's helper, as a pipefitter's helper, as an engineer's helper, when closely confined, on dirty work and on night work. Finally, he was "*poor*" as a machinist's helper, as a blacksmith's helper, as a carpenter's helper, at work requiring precision, on wet and cold jobs, when exposed to weather and when working in a variable temperature.

In the main, the statements as to the greater efficiency of white workers are empirical and based largely upon the experience which they have acquired at their jobs. No scientific data have been gathered on the relative efficiency of the white and the Negro worker.

In conclusion, it should be pointed out that the tragedy of human waste in industry is nowhere more outstanding than in the case of Negro employment. Blind alley occupations for workers who have latent capacity for other jobs is the rule rather than the exception among Negro workers. For the Negro there is little encouragement and less opportunity for promotion. Success stories of rises from laborer to superintendent and manager are few. Opportunities for training are even more restricted. Apprenticeships are few and other opportunities for trade training rare. Schools do not see the wisdom of training Negro pupils in skilled crafts because there is no opportunity for placing them after they have been trained. Employers will not hire them because they have no training. The vicious circle continues when a privileged few do receive the training or the required apprenticeship only to find that white workers refuse to accept them as fellow workmen. Strikes have been waged on this account. Union workers have been known to walk off the jobs when a Negro fellow unionist was employed.

TABLE VII

Index of Occupancy of All Workers and Negro Male Workers Employed in Broad Occupational Groups 1910 and 1920 and of Negro Males in These Specific Occupational Groupings—1910, 1920

A

BOTH SEXES

OCCUPATIONAL GROUP	1920 TOTAL	1920 NEGRO	1920 INDEX OF OCCUPANCY	1910 TOTAL	1910 NEGRO	1910 INDEX OF OCCUPANCY
1. Agriculture, Forestry, etc.	9,869,030	2,178,888	1.0166	12,659,203	2,893,375	1.4157
2. Extraction of Minerals	1,090,233	73,229	1.4154	964,824	61,129	0.3304
3. Manufacturing and Mechanical Industries	12,818,524	826,810	0.3574	10,658,881	631,280	0.3088
4. Transportation	3,063,582	312,421	0.5269	2,637,671	255,945	0.5060
5. Trade	4,242,979	140,467	0.1710	3,614,670	119,491	0.1724
6. Public Service (Not elsewhere specified)	770,460	50,552	0.3381	459,291	22,382	0.2541
7. Professional Service	2,143,889	80,183	0.1932	1,663,569	67,335	0.5391
8. Domestic and Personal Service	3,404,892	1,064,590	16.1561	3,772,174	1,122,262	15.5220
9. Clerical Occupations	3,126,541	37,011	0.0611	1,737,053	19,336	0.0581

MALES

OCCUPATIONAL GROUP	1920 TOTAL	1920 NEGRO	1920 INDEX OF OCCUPANCY	1910 TOTAL	1910 NEGRO	1910 INDEX OF OCCUPANCY
1. Agriculture, Forestry, etc.	10,953,158	1,566,627	1.6135	10,851,702	1,842,238	1.6066
2. Extraction of Minerals	1,087,359	72,892	0.6814	963,730	61,048	0.5975
3. Manufacturing and Mechanical Industries	10,888,183	781,827	0.7297	8,837,901	563,342	0.6010
4. Transportation	2,850,528	308,896	1.0997	2,531,075	254,654	0.9513
5. Trade	3,575,187	129,309	0.3676	3,146,582	112,464	0.3383
6. Public Service (Not elsewhere specified)	748,666	49,586	0.6466	445,733	22,043	0.4680
7. Professional Service	1,127,391	41,056	0.3426	929,684	37,690	0.3892
8. Domestic and Personal Service	1,217,968	273,959	2.2863	1,241,328	268,875	2.0505
9. Clerical Occupations	1,700,425	28,710	0.1716	1,143,820	16,204	0.1344

B

Index of Occupancy of Negro Workers in Selected Occupations—1920

Specific Occupations	Total Male Workers	Male Negro Workers	Index of Occupancy Male Negro Workers
Coal Mine Operatives	732,441	72,892	1,01159
Bakers	93,347	2,064	0.2249
Blacksmiths	221,416	8,886	0.4079
Boilermakers	74,088	1,398	0.1918
Brick and Stone Masons	131,257	10,606	0.8213
Carpenters	887,208	34,217	0.3920
Electricians	212,945	1,342	0.0640
Engineers, Stationary	242,064	6,352	0.2667
Furnacemen, Smeltering, etc.	40,800	3,235	0.8059
Laborers			
Clothing Industries	6,414	1,169	1.8526
Food Industries	143,397	24,638	1.8526
Iron and Steel	717,022	104,518	1.4753
Lumber and Furniture	309,874	103,154	3.3837
Cotton Mills	59,646	10,182	1.7352
Machinists, Millwrights, etc.	894,654	10,286	0.1168
Molders, Founders and Casters	123,668	6,634	0.5452
Painters, Glaziers, etc. (Building)	248,394	8,026	0.3284
Paper Hangers	18,338	943	0.5227
Plasterers	38,249	5,814	1.9028
Cement Finishers	7,621	1,265	1.6872
Plumbers, Gas and Steam Fitters	206,715	3,516	0.1730
Semi-skilled			
Chemical Industries	32,072	1,916	0.6072
Clothing	143,718	6,265	0.4430
Food	116,493	11,160	0.9737
Iron and Steel	632,161	22,916	0.3684
Other Metals	60,944	990	0.1653
Lumber and Furniture	150,079	8,654	0.5861
Cotton Mills	153,269	2,550	0.1691
Iron (Structural) Workers	18,836	196	0.1220
Longshoremen and Stevedores	85,605	27,206	3.2304
Conductors, Steam Railroad	74,539	33	0.0039
Locomotive Engineers	109,899	111	0.0102
Locomotive Firemen	91,345	6,506	0.7239
Mail Carriers	90,131	3,639	0.4104
Laborers, Steam Railroad	463,613	95,921	2.1031

The Negro is yet on the fringe of America's industrial life. He continues to be the marginal worker, except in some localities where Mexican labor is utilized. He remains, however, the ominous threat to American labor. Realizing that bemoaning his fate is of little avail, the Negro worker has employed strategies that have accelerated his progress, and in so doing has left open for debate many of the most widely accepted theories of racial inferiority and employment. He has effected this change through the following methods:

1—Personal or individual bargaining—by selling the individual workers to the employer, securing thereby positions for which that worker as a Negro would not be eligible.

2—Through competitive examination in which superior ability is demonstrated.

3—Through political influence and power.

4—By accepting segregated working and training facilities.

5—By greater utilization of public training facilities.

6—By "passing," that is, those workers who may do so—using their color—or lack of color as a passport to positions which they would not obtain if it were known that they were Negroes.

7—By strikebreaking—utilizing the opportunities presented by strikes to enter those industries where they were not formerly employed because of certain policies of the management or of the workers.

8—By collective bargaining—exerting a collective pressure upon the employer, and in many cases the union, with or without the cooperation of the white worker.

It is in connection with a few ramifications of the last two compensatory methods of industrial adjustment that this monograph will be concerned, particularly with the issues presented in the relationship of these workers to organized labor in America.

FEDERATED UNIONS AND THE ADMISSION OF NEGRO WORKERS

The first national federation of labor unions to deal with the problem of Negro workers was the National Labor Union at its initial session in 1866. This organization was a delegate body, consisting of representatives of local, state and national trade associations. At the first of its seven conventions this body declared that "the interests of the labor cause demand that all workingmen be included within its ranks, without regard to race or nationality; and the interests of the workingmen of America especially required that formation of trades' unions, eight hour leagues, and other organizations should be encouraged among the colored race; and that they be invited to cooperate with us in the general labor undertaking." At the 1867 convention in Chicago, President S. C. Whaley said "The emancipation of the slaves has placed us in a new position, and the question now arises, what labor position shall they now occupy? They will begin to learn and to think for themselves, and they will soon resort to mechanical pursuits and thus come in contact with white labor. It is necessary that they should not undermine it, therefore the best thing that they can do is to form trades unions, and thus work in harmony with the whites." [1]

Though a course of action had been suggested, the "Committee on Negro Labor" reported that while aware of the danger of Negro competition, it was believed inexpedient to take action and recommended that the subject be tabled until the next session. The convention adopted this recommendation. In 1869, at the Philadelphia session, Negro workers were admitted as delegates. Here we find the first denunciatory resolutions on color discrimination in trades unions. This convention openly urged Negro workers to organize and send delegates to the next congress. The convention likewise appointed a committee of five members including one Negro engineer from Maryland to organize the colored workmen of Pennsylvania into labor unions. No report was made at future conventions of this committee's work.

This effort on the part of the National Labor Union appeared to be no more than a benevolent gesture "with only moral force at its back" that might be easily disregarded and nullified by either a national or local union disinclined to favor organization among

---

[1] Address before National Labor Union, 1867. Reprinted in Commons & Andrews, Documentary History, Vol. IX, p. 160.

Negroes. The cigar-makers—organized as a highly skilled craft union—excluded Negroes by constitutional provision. Negro carpenters in New Haven, Conn., were not admitted to the union. In fact so varied and extensive were the exclusions either by constitutional provisions or tacit agreement that the first Negro protest crganization, The Negro National Labor Union, was organized. This organization at its first session in Washington, D. C., December 1869, in a memorial to Congress called the exclusion of Negro workers and apprentices from industries and trades unions "an insult to God, injury to us and disgrace to humanity." In 1871 the protest was continued and made more imperative when it advised white workmen that "As long as you persist therein we cannot fellowship with you in your struggle."

The Knights of Labor succeeded the National Labor Union and was in its structure and philosophy an entirely different labor organization. To the Knight of Labor the interests and viewpoints of all workers were the same. Consequently the organization endeavored to unite the various skills, crafts and industries into one unit. Because of this type of organization a large number of Negro workers were unionized. One of the largest unions in New Orleans of the Coopers International Union was a Negro Union (1879). The cigar-makers removed the Negro exclusion clause from their constitution (1879). Negro delegates attended conventions from District Assemblies in Richmond, Va., and Pittsburgh, Pa. It was also reported that in 1885 Negro workers were becoming affiliated with the Knights of Labor in all parts of the South.[1]

The growth of American industry called for a different type of labor body. Thus the Federation of Organized Trades and Labor Unions in 1881 was destined to be the real labor power in America. To this group, later known as the American Federation of Labor, passed the leadership of the American labor movement.

By successful tactics the Federation gained a strategic position. The skilled craftsman was supreme. The policy of the organzied worker and his union was to protect his skill, which was at a premium, and his craft, which was an art. Organization of the unskilled was considered ill-advised, for that group then would become dependent upon the skilled workers in the union. They worried about the unskilled only "when they (the skilled workers) were in danger of losing their advantages and places, due to the

---

[1] McNeil, George. The Labor Movement, p. 136.

unstinted competition of the unskilled, and they then develop a "labor as a whole attitude." [1]

However, the American Federation of Labor attempted to maintain the same liberal membership policy toward the Negroes that was fostered by the Knights of Labor. The pressure of organization routine between 1881 and 1890 kept racial difficulties in the background. It was not until 1890 that specific attention was given to the problems of color discrimination, despite the fact that a previous declaration was to the effect that associations which refused admission to Negroes would be excluded from membership in the Federation. Because of this edict, the International Association of Machinists, whose constitution limited membership to white persons, was refused admission until 1895 when the objectionable qualification was removed.

In 1890 the American Federation of Labor convention went on record as looking with disfavor "upon trades unions having provisions in their constitutions which exclude from membership persons on account of race or color." In 1893 the convention reaffirmed "as one of the cardinal principles of the labor movement that the working people must unite or organize, irrespective of creed, color, sex, nationality or politics". By 1897 the Federation was finding it necesary to refute charges to the effect that trades unions were obstructing the economic progress of Negroes by refusing them admission to their organizations. At the 1897 convention the Federation of Labor continued to reaffirm its declaration that, "it welcomes into its ranks all labor without regard to creed, color, race, sex or nationality and that its efforts have been and will continue to be to encourage the organization of those most needing its protection, whether in the North or South, East or West, white or black".

It was soon apparent that mere declarations were not remedying the actual situations faced by Negro workmen. In 1900 Samuel Gompers, President of the American Federation of Labor, suggested that the Federation encourage and organize local unions and separate central bodies of Negro workers. The convention endorsed this plan. In 1902 the Federation provided for the issuance of separate charters to Central Labor Unions, Local Unions and Federal Labor Unions composed of Negro workers exclusively. After 35 years organized labor was put-

---

[1] Ely, The Labor Movement, p. 83.

ting into effect a plan suggested by President Whaley of the National Labor Union in 1867. Though this action was increasing the segregation of Negro workers within the organized ranks, it was the most practical effort that the Federation had exerted in behalf of the Negro since its existence.

The A. F. of L. rested on its laurels until 1910 when another storm arose over the relationship of the Negro worker to that body. Samuel Gompers had been accused of reading the Negro out of the labor movement. To this accusation he replied that the Executive Council voted to invite the Negro worker to join its ranks along with all other races, and, "instead of reading the Negroes out of the labor movement, my contention, and the contention of the American Federation of Labor is to try to bring them into the organized labor move-- ment in our own country." In the four year period preceding the World War the Federation continued the organization of local and federal unions in direct affiliation, maintained three Negro organizers and manifested some interest in "protecting the interests of labor". Meanwhile unions composed of whites and Negroes were seemingly working in complete harmony.

The increased industrial activity attending the World War, the migration of Negro labor and the accompanying strides created a most chaotic situation in the ranks of the Federation between 1916-1920, its period of greatest growth. In the conventions of 1916, 1917 and 1918 because of the appearance of new Negro labor, the Federation decided that Negroes should be organized but created no machinery to permit the organization. As a result of the annual meeting of the National Urban League on Urban Conditions Among Negroes held in New York in 1918 and a subsequent conference with the Executive Council of the A. F. of L., a resolution from a group of Negro organizations was presented to the 1918 convention of the Federation. This resolution follows:

New York, June 6th, 1918.

Hon. Samuel Gompers, President of
American Federation of Labor,
Washington, D. C.

My dear Mr. Gompers:

We write to present suggestions for further cooperation between our committee and the American Federation of Labor as growing out of our recent conference in Washington.

First, we wish to place before you our understanding of your statement to us at the conclusion of the meeting, We quote you as follows; and will be glad for you to make any changes in the text as will make the statement more nearly conform to the ideas which you have in mind relative to the connections that should be established between white and Negro workingmen:

"We, the American Federation of Labor, welcome Negro workingmen to the ranks of organized labor. We should like to see more of them join us. The interests of workingmen, white and black, are common. Together we must fight unfair wages, unfair hours, and bad conditions of labor. At times it is difficult for the national organization to control the actions of local unions in difficulties arising within the trades in any particular community, inasmuch as the National body is made possible by the delegates appointed by the locals; but we can and will use our influence to break down prejudice, on account of race, color or previous condition of servitude, and hope that you will use your influence to show Negro workingmen the advantages of collective bargaining and the value of affiliation with the A. F. of L. But few people who are not thoroughly acquainted with the rapid growth of the Federation of Labor know of the large numbers of colored people who are already members of our organization. The unpleasant incidents in connection with efforts of colored men to get recognition in trades controlled by the American Federation of Labor have been aired and the good effects of wholesome and healthy relationship have not been given publicity; and for that reason, a general attitude of suspicion has been developed towards union labor on the part of colored working people; but I hope that out of this conference will spring a more cordial feeling of confidence in each other on the part of men who must work for a living."

We are willing to cooperate with the American Federation of Labor in bringing about the results of the recent conference, and would make the following suggestions and recommendations which, with your approval, we shall proceed to carry out to the best of our ability.

First, we suggest that you prepare a statement, along the lines of the quotation from you given above, and send it to us for approval and then to be given to the Negro press throughout the country as expressing your position on matters connected with the relationship beween Negroes and white workingmen.

This statement, in our judgment, should contain a clear exposition of the reasons why certain Internationals may exclude colored men as they do by constitutional provision and still be affiliated with the A. F. of L. whose declared principles are opposed to such discrimination. This we think necessary because that stated facts above alluded to will be familiar to the leaders among the colored people, particularly to editors and ministers whose cooperation it is essential to secure if the best results are to be obtained.

We would suggest further that you consider the expediency of recommending to such internationals as still exclude colored men that their constitutions be revised in this respect.

Second, that a qualified colored man to handle men and organize them be selected for employment as an organizer of the American Federation of Labor, his salary and expenses, of course, to be paid by the American Federation of Labor.

Third, that for the present we meet at least once a quarter to check up on the results of our cooperative activities and to plan for further extension of the work, if satisfactorily conducted.

Fourth, that you carry out your agreement to have your Executive Council voice an advanced position in its attitude towards the organization of Negro workingmen and have these sentiments endorsed by your St. Paul convention in June, and this action be given the widest possible publicity throughout the country.

We should be glad to hear from you at your earliest convenience as to the action taken by your Council on these recommendations with such other suggestions or recommendations as may occur to you.

Sincerely yours,

EUGENE KINCKLE JONES,
FRED R. MOORE.

For the following committee:

Dr. R. R. Moton, Principal of Tuskegee Institute.

Mr. John H. Shillady, Secretary of National Association for the Advancement of Colored People

Mr. Fred R. Moore, Editor of New York Age

Mr. Archibald Grimke, Washington Association for the Advancement of Colored People

Mr. Emmett J. Scott, Special Assistant to the Secretary of War

Mr. Eugene Kinckle Jones, Executive Secretary, National Urban League

Mr. Thomas Jesse Jones, Education Director, Phelps Stokes Fund

Dr. James H. Dillard, President of Jeannes Fund

Dr. George C. Hall, Vice President of the Executive Board, Chicago Urban League.

This resolution was referred to the Committee on Organization, which reported as follows:

"It is with pleasure we learn that leaders of the colored race realize the necessity of organizing the workers of that race into unions affiliated with the American Federation of Labor, and your committee recommends that the President of the American Federation of Labor and its Executive Council give special attention to organizing the colored wage workers in the future. We wish it understood, however, that in doing so no fault is or can be found with the work done in the past, but we believe that with the cooperation of the leaders of that race much better results can be accomplished."

This report was unanimously adopted.

The Atlantic City, N. J., convention in 1919 was faced with several pertinent suggestions from Negro delegates. Requests were made that the American Federation of Labor consider the application of a representative group for a Negro union with an international charter—or exert its influence on national and international unions having jurisdiction over Negro workers. Other resolutions asked for Negro organizers. Another lodged a complaint against the International Union of Metal Trades. Many resolutions called for a special committee to study the organized labor situation among Negro workers. Aside from recommending that where Internationals refuse membership to Negro workers the Federation should organize these workers in locals directly affiliated with the Federation, the resolutions committee of this convention hoped "to see the day when these organizations (those excluding Negro workers) will take a broader view of this matter."

The Local and Federal Labor Unions that had been organized by the Federation launched a most concerted attack upon the indifference of the Federation toward the Negro workers in the Montreal Convention of 1920. The most outstanding resolution was that submitted by various locals and Federal labor unions requesting of the Federation—

1—The launching of an educational campaign among white and Negro workingmen to convince them of the necessity of "bringing into the ranks of labor all men who work regardless of race, creed, or color."

2—Periodic conferences of white and colored leaders with the Executive Council of the Federation on questions affecting Negro labor.

3—The appointment of an Executive Secretary of a special committee for organizing Negro workers who would be located at the headquarters of the Federation in Washington.

4—That there be Negro organizers in all crafts whose duties would be to build up Negro membership.

When these resolutions were reported from the committee, it was recommended to strike out Sections 1 and 3, and to amend Section 4 to read that Negro organizers be appointed—where necessary—to organize Negro workers. Section 4 was finally referred to the Executive Council for action if the funds of the organization should permit.

The membership of ten unions in the American Federation of Labor denying membership to Negro workers either through provisions in their constitution or rituals, has been the subject of resolutions in all conventions to date. At Montreal in 1920, the Federation requested the Railway Clerks to remove the words "only white" from their constitution. The Railway Clerks failed to comply with the request and remained in the Federation until January 1926 when its charter was revoked because of a jurisdictional dispute with the International Brotherhood of Teamsters. That the Federation will ever be able to rid itself of these problems of race and labor seems unlikely. If internal problems of adjustment do not arise, the efforts of organizations interested in the adjustment of Negro workers constantly reminds the Federation of its pronouncements in favor of that group. Such an activity was the open letter to the Federation of Labor and other groups of organized labor by the National Association for the Advancement of Colored People in 1924. This letter proposed the establishment of an Interracial Labor Commission which would undertake—

1—To find out the exact attitude and practice of national labor bodies and labor unions toward Negroes, and of Negro labor toward unions.

2—To organize systematic propaganda against racial discrimination on the basis of these facts at the great labor meetings, and in local unions.

When in 1925 the Negro Labor Congress—an organization effort of the Communist (Workers) Party in America — had received the support and encouragement of many local labor leaders, the Federation, through its President, William Green, was forced to reassure itself and the Negro workers of its philosophy on the organization of Negro labor—its tactical approach and organization successes being to the contrary, notwithstanding. The following excerpts are taken from an editorial on "Negro Wage Earners" appearing in the American Federationist.[1]

"Misrepresentation and deception has been used to promote the World Negro Congress in Chicago in October"—Such an effort deserves the indignation it has received. It is bad enough to mislead those who have an equal opportunity to know, but to take advantage of *the weaknesses of those who have a moral right to our special care* is quite outside the pale of decency and ethics."—The A. F. of L. offers to Negro wage earners the protection and the experience of the trade union movement."

During 1925 and 1926, T. Arnold Hill of the Department of Industrial Relations of the National Urban League twice appeared before the Executive Council of the A. F. of L. with a suggested procedure for organizing Negro workers. While the Executive Council and President Green looked with favor upon the active interest shown in the cause of labor in general and Negro labor in particular, and, though the Executive Council gave "most thoughtful consideration" to the matter, the Federation could not undertake the expense involved in defraying *one-half* of the expenses of a colored organizer on the organizing staff of that body.

---

[1] Vol. 32, No. 10—October, 1925.

Meanwhile the Federation is engaged in an imbroglio with the Hotel and Restaurant Employees and Beverage Dispensers International Alliance in a jurisdictional dispute involving the newly organized Brotherhood of Sleeping Car Porters.

What then is the official position of the American Federation of Labor toward the organizing of Negro workers? It comprises a number of resolutions urging organization of Negro workers; a protest here and vacuous decrees there against efforts of radicals at organization; segregated organization of Negro workers in certain occupations through local and federal labor unions; a few pleas for organization; the employment at various times of a few Negro organizers; and a total inability, if not unwillingness to compel International Unions to remove from their constitutions Negro exclusion clauses, or suffer expulsion from the Federation.

The Federation essays certain policies, "stand for" them—realizing it cannot carry them out. It has attempted to live up to its philosophy of liberalism without performing the mechanics necessary to make that liberalism a reality. So vacuous and few have been its efforts in behalf of Negro workers despite its pronouncements, that it has failed to crystalize the opinion of Negro and white workers and the intelligent public to any other conclusion than that the American Federation of Labor "stands for" the organization of workers despite their race, creed or color, then with complacent self satisfaction "sits down," having actually done nothing. In fact, among Negro workers the American Federation of Labor because, of its "hands off" policy during the early nineties, and because of its failure to maintain the organziation of the thousands of Negro workers organized under local and federal labor unions in 1919, 1920, 1921, and 1922, has less power and influence among the Negro group than at any other time in its history. To quote Leo Wolman: "The American Federation of Labor as a central organizing machine had fallen into disuse for this purpose several decades ago, and as it grew older it lost, with its youth, its energy and initiative."[1]

Nevertheless, it must be admitted when a comparison is made between the policies of many of the international and local unions on the question of organizing Negroes and those of the American Federation of Labor, that the latter has had a more liberal official attitude than the Nationals and Internationals upon whom it depended for carrying into operation its official position.

---

[1] Wolman, Leo—"Economic Conditions and Union Policy" in American Labor Dynamics, p. 40.

THE NATIONAL AND INTERNATIONAL UNIONS

The strength of the American Federation of Labor rests upon the strength of the national and international unions. Many of these unions formed between 1880 and 1900 "totally misread the trends in American industry". Machinery, women, unskilled and semi-skilled workers and Negroes were subject to the restrictions of their constitutions and by-laws. Despite the entrance of women and Negroes into industrial fields, the inroads of machinery, and the division of processes, these unions failed to effect the changes necessary in their "organization machinery" to the task of admitting and holding in membership a highly industrialized working population quite different from the craftsmen who founded the great craft unions of the United States in the 70's, 80's and 90's.[1] Today no less than twenty-four national and international unions, ten of which are affiliated to the American Federation of Labor, exclude Negroes from their membership through provisions in their constitution or rituals. These unions are

METALS AND MACHINERY

*The International Brotherhood of Boilermakers, Iron Shipbuilders and Helpers of America.

*The International Association of Machinists.

TRANSPORTATION

*The Brotherhood of Railway Carmen.

*The Brotherhood of Railway and Steamship Clerks, Freight Handlers, Express and Station Employees.

The Brotherhood of Dining Car Conductors.

*The Order of Sleeping Car Conductors.

The Order of Railway Conductors of America.

The Grand International Brotherhood of Locomotive Engineers.

The Order of Railway Expressmen.

The American Federation of Express Workers.[2]

The Brotherhood of Locomotive Firemen and Enginemen.

---

[1] Ibid. p. 40.

* Affiliated to the American Federation of Labor.

[2] Now affiliated with Brotherhood of Railway Clerks.

*The National Organization of Masters, Mates and Pilots of North America.

The Neptune Association.

The American Federation of Railroad Workers.

*The Switchmen's Union of North America.

The Brotherhood of Railroad Trainmen.

The Brotherhood of Railroad Station Employees and Clerks.

The American Association of Train Despatchers.

The Railroad Yard Masters of North America.

The Railroad Yardmasters of America.

PUBLIC SERVICE

*Railway Mail Association.

MANUFACTURES

*The American Wire Weavers Protective Association

MISCELLANEOUS

*The Order of Railroad Telegraphers.

*The Commercial Telegraphers Union of America.

Because of the American Federation of Labor's policy that affiliated organizations may not retain in their constitutions any discriminatory clause or clauses against Negroes, the Boilermakers and the Machinists accomplish this exclusion by a pledge which forms a part of the ritual and binds each member to propose only white workmen for membership.[1]

The other unions affiliated with the Federation have not exercised the caution shown by the Machinists [2] and Boilermakers and retain the discriminatory clauses in their constitutions. The Railway Carmen limits its membership to "any white person between the ages of 16 and 65 years." Since 1921, however, this union has made a special ruling for some Negro workers. The

---

* Affiliated to the American Federation of Labor.

[1] Vide: Wolfe, F. E. Admission to American Trade Unions, 1912. Proceedings, Boilermakers and Iron Ship Builders, 1908, p. 494. Ritual, I. A. of Machinists, 1909, p. 5.

[2] At the 1920 convention of the International Association of Machinists seven (7) resolutions were introduced to remove the word "white" from the ritual. The convention voted down the proposition. These resolutions were introduced by representatives of locals from Chicago, Ill. (2) Columbia, S. C.; Akron, Ohio; New Haven, Conn.; Tuscon, Arizona. Resolutions opposing such action came from Bakersfield, California; Pine Bluff, Arkansas; Whistler, Alabama; and Savannah, Georgia.

general secretary-treasurer reports that the union does grant a restricted membership to 500 Negroes employed chiefly on railroads in the South. These Negro workers are organized in separate auxiliary bodies that function under the jurisdiction of the nearest white local or lodge. The 1921 convention of the Brotherhood adopted the following constitutional amendment:

"On railroads where the employment of colored persons has become a permanent institution they shall be admitted to membership in separate lodges. Where these lodges of Negroes are organized they shall be under the jurisdiction of the nearest white local, and shall be represented in any meeting of the Joint Protective Board Federation, meetings or conventions where delegates may be *seated* by white men."

Subject to the trade and territorial jurisdictional requirements the Railway and Steamship Clerks admit "all white persons". The Dining Car Conductors require that their members be of the "Caucasian race". The Sleeping Car Conductors restrict their membership to "white males, sober and industrious," while the Railway Conductors admit "any white man" who can satisfy the additional requirements. The Locomotive Engineers, Express Workers, Expressmen, Firemen and Enginemen, Railroad Workers, Switchmen, Railroad Telegraphers, Commercial Telegraphers, Train Dispatchers, Trainmen, both unions of Yardmasters, Masters, Mates and Pilots, and the Neptune Association specify that their members must be white. The Railroad Station Employees and Clerks, however, are more cautious in requiring that their members be "born of white parents". The Wire Weavers Protective Association not only requires that its members be "white" and "christian", but requires foreigners to pay an initiation fee of $1,000.

As a result of the exclusion policies of these unions not less than 225,000 Negro workers are denied trade union affiliation and its attendant benefits.

Contrasted with the national unions denying membership to Negroes are those unions which have denied them the full privileges of membership but do permit affiliation through auxiliary bodies. The International Brotherhood of Blacksmiths, Drop Forgers and Helpers was finally forced to organize Negro workers because of the serious inroads that group was making into the organized field. The union has sought to protect its craft from Negro usurpation by specifying that Negro members may not be promoted to blacksmiths or helper-apprentices. The special qualifications for colored members in the Brotherhood are:

"Where there are a sufficient number of colored helpers they may be organized as an auxiliary local and shall be under the jurisdiction of the white local having jurisdiction over that territory. Colored helpers shall not transfer except to another auxiliary local composed of *colored members, and colored members shall not be promoted to blacksmiths or helper apprentices, and will not be admitted to shops where white helpers are now employed.*"[1]

One of the objects of the Brotherhood of Blacksmiths, as stated in its constitution is "to perpetuate our association on the basis of friendship and justice." Approximately 10,000 Negroes are employed in the trades over which this union has jurisdiction, while only 300 are members of this union.

The Brotherhood of Maintenance of Way Employees has in its constitution a special provision for Negro members as follows: Colored workers "shall be entitled to all the benefits and protection guaranteed by the constitution to members and shall be represented in the grand lodge by delegates of their own choosing selected from any white lodge in the system division where they are employed. Nothing in this section operates to prevent colored employees from maintaining a separate lodge for social purposes."[2]

While it is difficult to estimate the exact number of Negro workers coming within the jurisdiction of this union, the fact that there are more than 115,000 Negro railroad workers in the United States, excluding 20,000 porters, is of interest. Of this number there are 202 inspectors of ways and structures, 1,195 foremen and overseers and 97,000 laborers and miscellaneous workers from whom the union recruits its restricted Negro membership.

The International Association of Sheet Metal Workers, maintaining jurisdiction over no more than 2,500 Negro sheet metal workers, provides in Article IV, Section 1 of its constitution that:

---

[1] Handbook of American Trade Unions, Bulletin of the U. S. Bureau of Labor Statistics, No. 506, p. 55, November, 1929.

[2] Ibid, p. 89.

"Where there are a sufficient number of Negro sheet metal workers, they may be organized under the regular charter of the International Association by conforming to Article IV, Section 3 of this constitution. Separate charters to Negro sheet metal workers will be granted only with the consent of the white local union established in the locality, where charter is applied for. Auxiliary locals of Negro sheet metal workers may be organized in localities where consent of the white local unions is not obtained and shall come under the jurisdiction of the white local union having jurisdiction over said locality. No member or members of Negro local unions or auxiliaries shall transfer into any other than a Negro local union or auxiliary affiliated to the Sheet Metal Workers' International Association."[1]

The Hotel and Restaurant Employees' International Alliance governs its colored members as follows:[2]

SECTION 19.

"If a member of a colored local moves to a city where no local of his craft or race exists, he shall remain a member of the local of the city from which he came."

SECTION 20.

"If a colored worker at our craft shall desire to enter a local in a city where only a white local exists, he may be accepted in the International Union as a member-at-large, provided he possesses the necessary qualifications."

SECTION 21.

"Candidates accepted under the above conditions shall be initiated by the local in the city where the candidate resides."

SECTION 96.

"Where there exists a white and (a) colored local in any city, they shall elect representatives to meet at least twice a year to equalize the scale of wages and conditions of employment of the craft."

There are other national organizations that have admitted Negroes with strings attached to the admission. Among these unions are the National Rural Letter Carriers Association and the National Federation of Rural Letter Carriers, the latter

---

[1] Article IV, Section 3, refers to the organization of more than one local in any locality or city.

[2] Vide: Constitution, Hotel and Restaurant Employees International Alliance, pp. 6, 7, 22.

being affiliated to the American Federation of Labor. In both of these organizations only white members are eligible as delegates to conventions and as office holders.

It is not to be assumed, however, that the absence of constitutional clauses discriminating against Negro workers implies their admission into these unions. Tacit agreement, examinations and local determination of eligibility for membership serve as deterrents to Negro inclusion in many unions. The Plumbers have never made an issue of the question of admitting Negroes, though it is generally understood that they are not admitted. Despite persistent efforts of Negro plumbers in Philadelphia, New York and Chicago to secure membership, they have not succeeded. Yet, a non-union Negro master plumber in New York may hire white union plumbers to work for him on a union job. In Philadelphia, the licensing board will not grant licenses to Negro plumbers. In Charleston, W. Va., Negro plumbers because of keen competition enjoy the same rights, privileges, wage scale and work conditions as white union plumbers, without belonging to the union.[1] There are approximately 4,500 Negro plumbers and apprentices in the United States.

The Electrical Workers maintain no constitutional clause regarding Negro membership—but no Negroes are known to be members of this union except in Chicago where there is one. The early attitude of this organization is reflected in the editorial appearing in the Electrical Workers Journal in 1903. The editor wrote: "We do not want the Negro in the INTERNATIONAL BROTHERHOOD OF ELECTRICAL WORKERS, but we think that they should be organized in locals of their own, affiliated to the American Federation of Labor as the organization knows no creed or color."[2]

Another instance of exclusion is that of the Flint Glass Workers who have no laws against Negroes, but who object to them universally "because the pipes on which glass is blown pass from one man's mouth to another."

Another factor enters into the situation in the case of the Railway Mail Association. The fact that the association is a non-commercial insurance society served as a reason for the exclusion of Negroes in 1911 while it was a member of the American Federation of Labor. "The reason for this change was the fact that the Negro members were found to be a poor insurance risk." However, the Railway Mail Association's attitude to Negro membership is more drastic than that of the commercial insurance companies.

---

[1] 1927.
[2] The Electrical Works—April, 1903, p. 102.

NEGRO MEMBERSHIP IN NATIONAL UNIONS

THE BUILDING TRADES

Among the unions of the building trades the Hod Carriers, Building and Common Larorers Union has by far the largest number of Negro members. Hod carrying for many years has been regarded as a Negro job. Very often, Negro masons and plasterers unable to secure work in their trades temporarily become hod-carriers. Because of the abundance of unskilled Negro labor in the building trades and because of the strength of organized labor in the building industry, approximately one-fifth of the 75,300 membership of this union is Negro. The two year investigation of Negro membership in this union revealed 10,131 members, one-third of whom were in the southern states. Strong locals, both of Negro, and Negro and whites, exist in the South as well as in northern cities. In New York, Chicago, Cleveland, Cincinnati, Detroit and Pittsburgh this union has been quite active. In Indianapolis, Indiana, the Local Union of Hod Carriers and Building Laborers erected a two-story business building costing $50,000 in 1929. More than three hundred Negroes are members and they form the only Negro union in the city of Indianapolis. Negro organizers are employed by the International Union, while several unions have Negro business agents. Many Negroes serve as delegates to the conventions held every five years. Problems of organization within this union are chiefly those of maintaining the wage and hour scale. Free competition is apparently greater among the building laborers than other organized groups. In many of the locals reporting, Negro membership was more than half of the total. The lack of work-interest on the part of members causes the turnover to be very high. There are 127,860 male Negro workers listed as building and general laborers in the 1920 census.

In 1886, five years after its organization, the United Brotherhood of Carpenters and Joiners modified its rules so that more than one charter might be granted in a local jurisdiction if the existing local union did not object.[1] A number of Negro carpenters in 1903 were denied admission to carpenters' unions in Atlantic City, N. J., and Birmingham, Ala. The extent of the international's remedy was limited to a recommendation that "the drawing

---

[1] Wolfe, p. 112-134.

of the color line should be stopped at once and for all times." In 1902 when efforts were made to appoint a Negro organizer, numerous objections were made, many persons expressing the opinion that under no conditions should a Negro be employed. The appointment of a Negro organizer was made and the opinion of the executive officer vindicated when in a period of ten years Negro organizers among the carpenters had organized in Southern States 25 locals of Negro carpenters exclusively.[1]

The principles of the Brotherhood include the following statement:

"We recognize that the interests of all classes of labor are identical, regardless of occupation, nationality, religion or color, for a wrong done to one is a wrong done to all."

To quote Frank Duffy, General Secretary:

"We organize colored men of the craft and have had quite a number of unions in the South. We found, however, below the Mason and Dixon Line that when we organized white and colored carpenters into a union, it did not last long. We then decided to organize them into separate local unions. That has been more satisfactory all around."

In 1926 the carpenters had 14 local unions of Negro carpenters with a membership of 642. All of these unions were in the South, yet in the North many colored members hold memberships in white local unions. Including the southern membership 1,572 Negroes were located in various locals of the Carpenters Union.

There are instances of local unions of carpenters not admitting Negro workers. Local No. 1242 (Cleveland, Ohio) composed of Parquet Floor Layers considered Negro membership undesirable and therefore refused to grant it, because "most of our work is in occupied dwellings the people (or customers) object to having a Negro working therein." When Negro carpenters apply to local No. 1456 in New York they are referred to No. 1888 which is composed of Negroes. In Harrisburg, Pa., the members of Local No. 287, "will not have both races in one local." In Philadelphia, Local No. 2066 composed entirely of Negro carpenters was organized because "Negro carpenters are not justly treated in mixed locals. Most Negro carpenters work on separate jobs from white carpenters in Philadelphia." The separate local of Negro carpenters (No. 92) in Mobile, Alabama, is not friendly with the white local of carpenters because the fact that the "Negro is said

---

[1] Harris and Spero, "The Negro in the American Labor Movement."

to do more work in a day causes jealousy on the part of the whites."

The object of the BRICKLAYERS, MASONS AND PLASTERERS INTERNATIONAL OF AMERICA is "to unite into one parent body, for mutual protection and benefit, all members of the mason craft that work at the same, who are citizens of the country within its jurisdiction, without condition as to servitude or race."

The Bricklayers did not affiliate with the American Federation of Labor until 1916. Ever since 1875 its approach to the problem of Negro masons had been a vacillating one. In 1870 the president of the union had recommended that the national body be empowered to charter more than one local in a locality which would permit the organization of Negro workers in cities where white locals refused them membership. In 1875 the laws of the union were altered to prevent such a step. In 1876 the convention voted against the organization of Negro workers. For seven years the situation remained unchanged. In 1881 the president reported a second decision in which the right of a Negro member to admission by card into any local union was held subject to local discretion. In 1883 and 1884 the recommendation for separate charters to Negroes on the approval of the executive board was approved when submitted to the subordinate unions. Nevertheless the opposition was so strong that the general secretary reported to the 1884 convention "through a mutual understanding between the members of the executive board it was deemed best not to exercise the power vested in them."

The absence of a specific rule in this case led to the assumption that Negro workers only rarely were admitted. By 1893 the International had evidently changed its policy, for the next year an independent local union of Bricklayers in Philadelphia would not affiliate with the National union because it wished to exclude Negroes.[1] In 1902 a union of bricklayers in Dallas, Texas, which had debarred Negroes for more than two years was ordered by the international body to eliminate the restrictive clause from its constitution. The national union two years later disapproved a similar situation in Sumter, S. C. The Bricklayer's Union was forced to provide in 1903, that, when a subordinate union would not agree to the granting of a charter to a new local union simply on account of "race, nationality or religion," the executive board would have discretionary power to grant the charter.

---

[1] Wolfe, op. cit.

Moreover, the national body has enforced the recognition of Negro members by establishing a fine for discrimination on account of race. In 1903 when the Indianapolis union discriminated against a Negro bricklayer having a transfer card, by accepting his card and then permitting the white workers to walk off the job when he reported to work, the union was fined $100. The next year Louisville, Cincinnati and Indianapolis unions debarred a Negro member possessing a travelling card, thereby provoking an opinion from the national secretary in 1905 to the effect that discrimination against Negroes 'had retarded the organization's progress.

ARTICLE XVII, Sec. 13, p. 69 of the present constitution provides: "A fine of One Hundred Dollars ($100) shall be imposed on any member or union who shall be guilty of discrimination against any member of the B., M. and P. I. U. by reason of race or color."

In 1926 ten locals in Southern States, Augusta, Savannah, Macon and Atlanta, Georgia; Jacksonville, Florida; Charleston, Columbia and Aiken, S. C.; Raleigh, N. C.; and Montgomery, Alabama; reported mixed locals of white and Negro members in which the Negro members were in the majority.

Though the international did not reply to the query on Negro membership, 1917 Negro members were located in 147 locals. In Local Union No. 1, of Birmingham, Alabama, whites and Negroes belong to the same union, and attend the same meetings, provisions being made on one side of the hall for the seating of the Negro members. It appears to be an unwritten law in Birmingham that white and Negro masons must not work together. The net result is that Negro unionists secure work wherever they can. Negro masons are reported as being quite discouraged over the situation.

The Negro brickmasons in Atlanta (Local No. 6), formerly were affiliated with white masons, who withdrew to form their own local. While white non-union bricklayers work with colored brickmasons, the white union mason will not work on the same jobs with colored masons. It was reported that Local No. 14, the white union, was disbanded (April, 1928), because of its attitude toward the colored union. Non-union Negro masons, it seems, prefer to remain unorganized at a wage scale 25 cents less on the hour than that demanded by the union.

Despite the fact that the relations between white and Negro members of Local No. 8, of Pensacola, Florida, are most cordial in meetings and on the streets, "whenever a Negro worker goes to a job and applies for work the answer is we are filled up." The majority of contractors in Pensacola are said to be "of the middle class of citizens, financially, and do not appear willing to see a Negro earn the union scale of wages."

In the past ten years there have been approximately 14 Negro bricklayers in Zanesville, Ohio, but all of them have either scabbed and were dropped, or transferred to other unions.

The Minneapolis, Minnesota local of brickmasons has only one Negro member. When Negro masons working on non-union jobs were approached for organization it was found that they were not qualified mechanics.

Everywhere there appears to be a problem. "Carelessness" of colored masons is the problem of Local No. 9, Charlotte, N. C., says the secretary. "Employers won't pay Negroes the union scale" comes as a complaint from union officials in cities North and South. Negroes are admitted on the same terms to Local No. 1 of Tennessee in Memphis, but are not treated alike within the local. In this instance whites are given the preference of work and they in turn refuse to work with Negroes. Finally, in Schenectady, N. Y., where Negroes and whites work together and belong to the same union, the opinion prevails that Negro workers should not be organized in separate locals from the white mechanics.

In the OPERATIVE PLASTERERS' AND CEMENT FINISHERS' INTERNATIONAL ASSOCIATION were found 782 Negro members distributed in 60 local unions. In 1920 there were 7,079 Negro males working as plasterers and cement finishers. The International organization has "sent an organizer through the country and there never was a question about who he organized so long as the men were competent plasterers or cement finishers." Furthermore, the constitution of this union provides that "any member or members that refuse to work with any other member in good standing in this association on account of his race, creed or nationality, thereby causing him to lose his job when such charges can be proven to the satisfaction of the Executive Board, he or they shall be fined the sum of One Hundred Dollars." [1] Such a clause, however, does not prevent a local organization, whose autonomy is not

---

[1] Constitution, Operative Plasterers and Cement Finishers, Sec. 54, p. 15.

defined in the International's constitution, from barring Negroes from membership. In Pittsburgh, Negro plasterers cannot join the white local, nor may they establish a local of their own.

Because of the monopoly Negro workers formerly held as plasterers in the South, many of the organizations are composed of white and Negro members. Local No. 62, (Negro) of Birmingham, Alabama, was organized in 1888, and in 1928 had a membership of 100. This union was once composed of Negro and white workers, but the Negro workers withdrew and secured a separate charter in 1926, because they preferred having their own local. In Montgomery, Alabama, where Negro workers were 35 of the 43 members, the white workers are given the preference in employment. The Philadelphia, Pennsylvania Local No. 592 won a strike in May, 1926, largely because it organized the Negro strikebreakers. The plasterers of Long Island, New York, regard the 30 Negro members in Local No. 759 as "absolutely essential to the movement." The Youngstown, Ohio, Local No. 179 had to admit Negro strikebreakers at $10.00 apiece in 1921 to win an open-shop struggle. The twenty Negro workers now in that union work harmoniously with the whites.

In 1920, 10,600 Negroes were employed as painters and decorators. Despite this fact the BROTHERHOOD OF PAINTERS, DECORATORS AND PAPERHANGERS OF AMERICA had only 279 members in separate locals in 1926. The total number of Negro painters located in the painters union was 718.

Many reasons have been given for the small Negro membership, the most general being that Negro painters did not meet the trade qualifications. Such a generalization, however, takes second place to the reasons offered by the statistician of Local Union No. 9, Kansas City, Missouri. Negro membership is undesirable there because of a "traditional bias by charter members, dating thirty-five years back." The union did make an effort "a while back" to organize a local union of painters, but "it seemed that not a sufficient number of them were working at our trade here to make it practicable.[1] Our general constitution does not prohibit the acceptance of Negro members, it is a matter for local action."

To carry on. There are 200 Negro painters in Chicago unions. A Negro painter has never been admitted to membership in any

[1] The 1920 Federal Census enumerates 37 Negro painters and paperhangers in Kansas City.

local in the jurisdiction of District Council No. 1, Pittsburgh, Pa. The secretary of Union No. 457 attributes as the cause for this "perhaps prejudice." Despite this statement Local No. 18 of the painters in Pittsburgh in 1925 was composed entirely of Negro painters numbering 65. The organization had five apprentices.[1] The admission of Negroes is "contrary to the *sentiment*" of local No. 79 of Denver. Never in twenty-seven years has the Paperhangers Local No. 128 of Cleveland had a Negro member, and there is a storm of protest each time the question is brought on the floor." Why?—one asks. Because they "do not desire the close association which would naturally be expected." Strikes have not influenced this lack of relationship; rather the "fear of the personal contact." The 1920 census showed only 52 Negro painters and paperhangers in Cleveland. In Chicago, the majority of Negroes are in a separate local while the others are distributed in locals throughout the city. In Buffalo, New York, Negroes are not admitted because "they would not be welcome in the homes." The Minneapolis Local No. 586 has no Negro members; believes Negroes make good union men, but "mixing them with whites is not a success in the North." In Pueblo, Colorado, the painters, decorators and paperhangers "do not care to associate with them (Negroes) as our equals." Negroes formerly refused to join Local No. 970 in Charleston, W. Va., which now has 3 Negro members out of 140, because the white painters refused them membership a few years ago. In Charleston, S. C., the colored painters are reputed to "keep their cards" better than the whites, and have better meetings. Local No. 139 in Charleston, a colored union was organized in 1901. In Jacksonville, Florida, the colored painters are organized into a separate Local No. 162. Both white and colored painters seem to respect union standards in so far as they are applicable to the local situation. Negro painters are permitted to work only within a certain territory.

No Negroes belong to THE INTERNATIONAL UNION OF ELEVATOR CONSTRUCTORS "because of the fact that none have ever applied." The Elevator Starters Union, which is affiliated with this body, had 10 Negro members in a total of 1,000 in 1926. That the organization has faced serious handicaps in endeavoring to organize Negro workers is seen in the following statements:

"The general attitude of the Negro in this Craft seems to be very unfavorable. We have worked in vain trying to

---

[1] Reid, Ira De A. The Negro in the Major Industries and Building Trades of Pittsburgh. 1925.

organize the Negro Elevator Operators. I have little or no use for the West Indian Negro. They are troublemakers. I have known of cases where they have offered to work for less money and actually rob a job from the non-union American Negro. I know of another case when he had men all lined up for organizing, and suddenly they changed their attitudes as to joining the union. We are at a loss to know just what caused this sudden change. On investigation we found two of the group were West Indians and had persuaded the others not to join the Union. We have recently tried to organize the group of Negro operators in the Daily News Building, all attempts have been very unsuccessful. We are having an outing this month, inviting all Negro operators, in fact we are urging them to join us with their families. At this time we are going to try to do some effective work. We are only successful at times when a non-union man is employed where there are all union men. We have very little trouble at this time winning them over. The Negro will not pay his dues in spite of our urging. In other words, they will not take the Union seriously."

Frank Crosswaith, Negro, who was organizer for the Elevator Starters and Operators Union says:

"When the Union came to realize not long ago that about 60% of the operators of the city were colored and that their membership among this group was negligible, they knew that union wages and for themselves were dependent upon securing union wages and conditions for the larger number of colored workers. Within a few months the Negro membership increased from 20 to 500, then later at a meeting attended by less than 25 Negroes, amidst much applause, Mr. Crosswaith was elected the Vice-president of the Union. Three weeks later, the secretary-treasurer, who was the wife of the white organizer "discovered" an error in the election. In the contest which followed, Mr. Crosswaith lost by six votes. He then resigned as Organizer and, incidentally, the Negro membership lapsed. The Negroes, however, seldom attend union meetings even to the meeting where their organizer was fighting to return to his office. Two explanations are offered for this. First, that the meetings were held in the Lower East Side, very far from Harlem where the majority of Negroes lived. The white men that attended lived near by. In the second place, Negroes were not welcome at union headquarters when they came in search of employment. They were always told to see the Negro Organizer, who was seldom in the office. Colored men were assured that no one in the office could help them, while white men that came were welcomed and encouraged even when work was unavailable. The colored membership of this union dropped to about 10."

Negro workers are admitted to full membership in the INTERNATIONAL UNION OF STEAM AND OPERATING ENGINEERS according to the general secretary-treasurer. Approximately 1,200 Negro workers are members of this union. The general character of Negro membership has been most satisfactory.

In specific instances, however, Negro workers have had to overcome local prejudices as in Pittsburgh.[1] Negroes were admitted to the Hoisting Engineers Union No. 66 because of the fierce competition they gave that union as non-union workers from 1901 to 1908. When a Negro engineer from Boston was unable to secure admission to this local, he started a union of colored workers that made serious inroads into Local No. 66's jurisdiction, securing desirable contracts that otherwise would have gone to that local. For ten years after the admission of Negroes into the union the two races worked harmoniously. In the period following the World War dissension arose and a movement launched to exclude Negroes and immigrants resulted in the establishment of a "lily white" Local No. 889.

The problem in a New York local is different. Says the secretary of this local:

In regards to Negroes in our line, it is impractical as we go up in office buildings and factories and repair much equipment. In many cases tenants would claim it repulsive. As for instance in the department store, have a Negro repairing a light back of a counter with four or five pretty white girls,— what the results would be! Figure it out!

The relations between white and Negro workers in Philadelphia are "splendid." Mixed smokers are held and games played together. It is not much trouble organizing them, but hard to keep them organized.

The INTERNATIONAL ASSOCIATION OF BRIDGE STRUCTURAL AND ORNAMENTAL IRON WORKERS admits Negro workers on parity with white workers. Few Negroes are engaged in structural iron work. Three Negroes who belonged to the Pittsburgh, Pennsylvania local brought transfer cards from other cities and were working on small jobs in that vicinity. Where there is great danger, and a possibility of racial friction, Negro workers are not employed. The risks are too great.

---

[1] Ibid.

"No one shall be discriminated against for race or color" in the WOOD, WIRE AND METAL LATHERS' INTERNATIONAL UNION. The fact that the qualifications for membership are discretionary with local unions may partially account for there being no more than 200 organized Negro lathers in this union. In Pittsburgh the Lathers Union No. 33 was the only mixed union of the building trades having colored apprentices. In 1925 there were 3 Negro apprentices in a total of 22. The only Negro Metal Lather in the city was requested to affiliate with the union.

Among the other unions in the Building Trades reporting on Negro membership was the JOURNEYMEN STONE CUTTERS ASSOCIATION which has had 2 Negro members, both of whom had severed their affiliation, one to become a union employer in Manhattan, Kansas. The GRANITE CUTTERS ASSOCIATION has only 2 negro members in a total of 8,500. "Because of the fact that there are practically no Negroes working at our trade we have not made any effort to organize Negroes." The ASBESTOS WORKERS AND THE MARBLE, STONE AND SLATE POLISHERS reported no Negro members. THE SLATE, TILE AND COMPOSITION ROOFERS reported 19 Negro members. In the INTERNATIONAL BROTHERHOOD OF STEAM SHOVEL AND DREDGEMEN there were 15 Negro members.[1]

TRANSPORTATION

Because the unions of railway agents, railway carmen, railway and steamship clerks, freight handlers, express and station employees, railway conductors, dining car conductors, sleeping car conductors, locomotive engineers, railway expressmen, express workers, locomotive firemen and enginemen, railroad workers, railroad station employees and clerks, railroad telegraphers, railroad trainmen, train dispatchers, railroad yardmasters (two unions), masters, mates and pilots, and the Neptune Association specifically exclude Negro workers, the Negro membership in this group of unions is restricted to a greater extent than in any other. The only transportation unions having an appreciable number of Negro members are the longshoremen, the tunnel and subway constructors[2] and the teamsters' unions.

The estimate that one-third of the 37,100 members of the INTERNATIONAL LONGSHOREMEN'S ASSOCIATION are Negroes was fairly substantiated by the findings of this study. In 23 locals

---

[1] In 1927 this union amalgamated with the International Union of Operative Engineers.

[2] Merged with International Hod Carriers, Building and Common Laborers Union in 1929.

5,381 of the 9,151 members were Negroes. New York City reports 1,200 additional Negro members. Negroes have taken an active part in the deliberations of the conventions, and have served on the executive council of the organization. In 1928 three of the fifteen national vice presidents of this organization were said to be Negroes, one of whom was Third Vice-President.

During the early days of the association there were constant difficulties between white and Negro longshoremen. Many strikes were broken with Negro workers. It was not until 1910 that any serious efforts were made to organize the Negro long-shoremen. The success with which the organization has been carried on is shown in the fact that there were only 27,000 Negro longshoremen and stevedores in 1920. In 1926 there were 40 Negro locals of the I. L. A. and 2 locals where the membership was equally divided.

Vice President Ryan of the I. L. A. has expressed himself as being opposed to separate locals. It appears that the spread of this type of organization has tended to develop an independence on the part of locals which at many times has caused friction: "I have recommended many times to keep such locals as far as possible from trying to make themselves too independent by only admitting certain nationalities. A type of the strong Negro local is No. 968 in Brooklyn, claiming 1,200 members of whom 1,000 are Negroes, as are all of the officers. This organization founded by Negroes and whites, successfully defended the organization from those agitators who sought to raise a color issue. Though white members keep up their dues they seldom attend the meetings. One advantage of the mixed local has been in this instance to stop white longshoremen from calling Negro workers "nigger". The local has been unsuccessful in endeavoring to have the International Association appoint a Negro organizer. The Negro strikebreaker among longshoremen in New York is always an ominous threat. As late as 1919 employers successfully used such a group of workers.

In Baltimore, Local No. 921 has 45 Negro members in its total roster of 150. They meet together and the relations are most cordial. Local No. 829 in the same city with a total membership of 900 has 175 Negro members. Until 1912 practically all the longshoremen on the Baltimore waterfront were Germans. They had formed the Baltimore Longshoremen's Association. A strike in 1912 caused the shippers to successfully employ imported Negro longshoremen from Norfolk, Va. The Negro workers were given ample protection so that no serious trouble occurred between them and the German workers. As a result of this strike, an organizer of the I. L. A. was sent in to unionize the longshoremen. Apparently, because of the dislike and suspicion existing between the white and the colored longshoremen only the white workers were to be organized. The plan was frustrated because the shippers refused to recognize the white union workers unless the Negro workers were organized as well. Following this impasse the I. L. A. began to organize both white and colored workers. The two races have maintained a workable relationship in this union, despite the fact that some of the colored members withdrew in 1916 to form another local, because of what was said to be "the questionable honesty of certain white financial officers on the controlling board of the union."

In Newport News and Norfolk, Virginia, active locals of colored longshoremen are reported. The 1,200 colored longshoremen in the Hampton Roads district receive 80 cents per hour for straight time, 85 cents per hour for overtime, and double time for holidays and Sunday. In New Orleans where once the largest number of Negro longshoremen was located, the Negro unions have gradually lost ground. According to Edward Gurtnet, delegate from Local No. 426 to the Central Trades and Labor Council, there are 4,000 Negroes and 500 whites in the Longshoremen's union.[1] The unfavorable working conditions in Charleston, S. C., have caused the membership of Local No. 188 to drop from 700 to 200. In Orange, Texas, the Negro and white members meet in separate halls, but on any matters of importance joint meetings are held. Negro members were taken into the Pensacola, Florida, Local No. 1089 but they would not stick. On October 1, 1923 the local had a membership of 600. In July 1926 the total membership was 65 of whom 25 were colored. The secretary of that local writes:

"The Negro makes a good union man as long as everything goes on smooth, but when the time comes to demand his rights and stand by his oath and obligation he has all kinds of excuses—his house rent is due, his furniture bill is due, his family is suffering. his meal barrel is empty— and so on. And then he stands up before the body and takes on oath that he is going to stand pat and that his whiskers would touch the ground before he would go back to work. Nine times out of ten some of the men the very next day would report to the organization that this same brother had flew the coop and went back to work. His whiskers sure did grow fast. This continued until our membership dwindled down to about 40 white and 25 colored who are still loyal to the organization."

---

[1] Associated Negro Press Dispatch, July 24, 1926.

In Brunswick, Georgia, "work is so scarce that there is little need" for the existing organization. In San Diego, California, Negroes, Mexicans and whites form Local No. 389. Approximately 50 per cent of the membership is Mexican. There are 11 Negro members and absolutely no friction.

Philadelphia has had a most interesting development of the Longshoremen Union. Local No. 1116 with 3,000 members, of whom 1,500 are Negroes, was formerly part of I. W. W. organization on the Philadelphia waterfront. Between 1913 and 1920 some 2,000 Negroes belonged to the union. The 1922 strike of the I. W. W. was broken by Negro strikebreakers. To destroy the I. W. W. in its campaign for an 8-hour day and other changes in work conditions, it was held by union officials that employers and certain labor leaders "conspired" to accomplish this by pitting the Negroes against the whites. As the strike was lost the I. W. W. organization was destroyed. There was no strong longshoremen's organization until 1926, when Local No. 1116 was organized.

The INTERNATIONAL SEAMEN'S UNION of America accepts Negro seamen to membership but gives no report on the number of members The last big strike conducted by the union in 1921 involved both races. Negro strikebreakers have been used very often but "the failure of Negroes to respond to organization has hampered the union more than the actual services of Negro strikebreakers." Yet, Andrew Furuseth, President of the Seamen's Union is quoted as saying on the question of Negro and white memberships: "We found that having common clubrooms for both, they would not mix. Sailing together in the same vessel would cause eternal trouble, and the Negro was as impossible as the white, if not more so. Our organization was never hostile to Negroes, and is not now. The employment on the same vessel, in the same department, however, has been found impossible for two reasons. (1) The Negroes protest and (2) the whites protest. and we do not know which is the one that protests the loudest and the most effectively."

The SAILORS UNION OF THE PACIFIC with headquarters in San Francisco and 2,700 members, none of whom are Negroes, has had "poor success" in securing Negro memberships. The SAILORS UNION OF THE GREAT LAKES has no Negro members, but does not exclude them. The union, however, is not in a position to state "just what stand the vessel owners would take in the matter of employing Negro seamen." The MARINE COOKS AND STEWARDS

UNION OF THE GREAT LAKES has a "considerable number" of Negroes in its organization. The FERRY BOATMEN'S UNION OF CALIFORNIA has 4 Negroes in its membership of 800. When the organization was formed in 1918 there were 6 Negro cabin watchmen on the Northwestern Pacific Company ferries, operating between San Francisco and Sausalito, California. They formed the union, and one of the first victories was eliminating the discriminating wage paid "these Negroes ($98.70 per month as compared with white cabin watchmen on the S. P. ferries who received $105.75). The monthly wage for all ferrymen was increased to $129.40 in 1926. Nevertheless, for some unexplainable reason these men. with one or two notable exceptions, after having been received on an absolute parity and one of them holding a high office in a 99 per cent white union, have seen fit to drop out. Even the four we are crediting as members with one exception are consistently from six months to one year or more in arrears."

In canvassing one-eighth of the membership of the INTERNATIONAL BROTHERHOOD OF TEAMSTERS, CHAUFFEURS, STABLEMEN AND HELPERS OF AMERICA only 313 Negro members were found. Locals are divided according to the kind of service rendered in large centers. The largest memberships are found in Illinois, California, Massachusetts, New York and Ohio. The largest Negro memberhip is found in Illinois. In Cincinnati, O. approximately 150 Negroes belong to Local No. 108, the City and Sanitary Drivers and Helper's Union. The Milk Wagon Drivers, Chauffeurs and Dairy Employees Union No. 98 in the same city reports 75 Negro members. The Minneapolis Local of the same type of service has one Negro. In Chicago the three Negroes who belong to the Milk Wagon Drivers' Union are used for trucking milk. Negroes and whites belong to the same union in Newark, though the former are reported as being "dense and must be pushed to progress".

THE AMALGAMATED ASSOCIATION OF STREET AND ELECTRIC RAILWAY EMPLOYEES OF AMERICA reports 16 Negro members. The Negro membership in Detroit where Negroes are employed on the surface cars, is unknown. In Trenton, New Jersey, there are 15 Negro members, 14 of whom are employed at the power house and one as a track greaser. In Boston, Mass., where a Negro was employed on the Elevated Railway the members of the local union protested his appointment and refused to take him out on the cars, with the result that inspectors and other officials had to give the instruction. When the matter was brought to the attenion of President Mahon of the International Union he ruled that the Negro conductor should not be discriminated against, and that he was entitled to join the union.[1]

The INTERNATIONAL UNION OF SUBWAY CONSTRUCTORS admits Negroes to full membership. With a Negro organizer operating in New York the union has brought in approximately 600 Negro workers.

In the early years of the RAILWAY MAIL ASSOCIATION Negroes were admitted to membership.[2] The exclusion of this group in later years left 6 Negro members in the Kansas City (Mo.) Branch of the Association, who are classified as "holdovers". The Secretary of this branch writes: "Our organization is against the employment of Negroes in the Railway Mail Service but this of course is a matter that is entirely up to Congress and the Post Office Department." In Charleston, South Carolina, however, there exists a Railway Mail Clerks Union of 145 members, 15 per cent of whom are Negroes. These members get along well together in a thriving organization. (It was impossible to determine whether this union was a branch of the Railway Mail Association.)

In 1922 R. H. Lewis, a Negro clerk in the Railway Postal Service for twenty years was appointed clerk in charge of one of the railway lines. As a result of this appointment the Richmond (Va.) Branch of the Railway Mail Association passed the following resolution:

At a meeting of the Richmond Branch, Railway Mail Association, held on November 11, the following resolutions were passed:

Whereas, the Post Office Department has seen fit to appoint R. H. Lewis, a Negro, to the position of Clerk-in-Charge on the Washington and Charleston R. P. O., which is considered a white line; therefore be it,

Resolved, by the Richmond Branch Railway Mail Association, that we go on record protesting against the above appointment and that this resolution be spread on the minutes and copies sent to Second Assistant Postmaster General, General Superintendent, our National Officers, Senators Glass and Swanson, and Congressman Montague.

(Signed)   J. N. BALDWIN, *President.*

[1] Baltimore Afro-American, February 6, 1926.

[2] Fifteen years ago there were 200 Negro clerks who were members of the Railway Mail Association.

[53]

This matter, and that of the exclusion of Negro workers from the Railway Mail Association because of the insurance features, was brought to the attention of President Collins of the R. M. A. by an interested fellow worker, also a Negro. In reply the following letter was received.

RAILWAY MAIL ASSOCIATION

Executive Offices

A. F. of L. Building, Washington, D. C.

Washington, D. C., Feb. 25, 1923.

Dear Sir:—

Your letter referring to the action of the Richmond Branch in adopting the resolution protesting the appointment of R. H. Lewis to the position of clerk in charge on the Washington & Charleston at hand.

I note that you take exception to the provisions of the constitution of the Railway Mail Association. The National Convention of the Association is the supreme legislative body of the organization and has ample authority to amend the constitution in any way it thought advisable not in conflict with the fraternal insurance laws.

The action taken by the National Convention was well founded. Statistics indicate that certain groups of society are a greater risk than other groups. Being chartered as a fraternal organization it was inconsistent for the Association to attempt to carry any group of workers at the expense of others and this thought possibly had a great deal to do with the amending of the constitution as it was amended.

I am not in a position to comment upon the promotion of Mr. Lewis. If the departmental officials see fit to make such promotion under the rules now in effect, then we all can reserve the right to criticize their judgment. It is a well known fact that the best results are obtained by harmony among the workers and the clerks of the Richmond Branch feel that harmony and respect will not obtain by the promotion of Mr. Lewis to the position of clerk in charge.

Respectfully,

(Signed)   W. M. COLLINS, *President.*

The organization problems of Negro workers engaged in Railway Transportation have been partially met by the institution of

Negro unions, erstwhile "protest" organizations. The following statement by a Negro organizer of these unions gives the slant of the Negro worker on the existing conditions.

"The clauses in certain contracts governing the employment of colored men as railway trainmen or train porters, where it is specified that to have full trainmen's rights a porter or other employe must have had a given number of months service (usually three months) in freight service, has had several harmful results on the colored "head-end" trainmen, commonly called "train porters." First, since the dominant organization holding the vast majority of such jobs on practically all railroads is the Brotherhood of Railway Trainmen, which does not accept Negroes to membership, it is apparent, that under their contracts, Negroes can have no status as trainmen in passenger service because they cannot begin work as freight service men. Next, many roads now having colored freight trainmen have not hired any colored men for over ten years, hence on such roads no colored man hired during that time could transfer to passenger service with a trainman's rating under terms of the standard contracts. Also, colored men hired for passenger train service must take the rating, pay and working conditions of the particular road assigned to train porters."

On many roads colored men with freight train records enjoy seniority as to assignments and identical treatment as to pay and working conditions generally given whites. However, the most flagrant abuses directed towards colored men are found under these very conditions. Since colored men cannot act as flagmen on "rear ends" of trains in many of the states where they have trainmen's ratings, it is common practice for a senior white man to exercise his rights to the "head end" of the train and displace the colored man, say of twelve years service, with freight experience while he, the white man, with no more than six months or a year's service, can and does take the flagging job. Therefore, the Negro must "bump" a junior Negro or "hit the extra boards" which means at least temporary unemployment. Another result of this situation is that Negroes when employed as train porters must work for less pay and possibly longer hours although in any instance at the direction of the train conductor, the so-called porter performs regularly designated trainman's duties. "This was made a rule by the Southeastern Federal Regional Director under the Railway Administration of the government." For obvious reasons the number of train porters increased in the years immediately following 1919. Also, the number of Negro trainmen decreased.

"Immediately following the World War, and owing principally to the equalization of pay and working conditions, there was a decrease in the number of jobs for colored locomotive firemen and enginemen on many of the roads. After the wartime wage rates went into effect and because of the regularity of the employment, the white men went after these jobs and are still after them." Yet, the efficiency of the Negro locomotive fireman is seldom questioned. Certainly never because of his race or color. In fact he is admitted to excel under many conditions by many of his employers. However, regularity of employment and high wages coupled with the fact that grades have been lowered, curves straightened, machinery made more efficient, oil taking the place of coal and in addition the abnormal and perverse social viewpoint that Negroes can live on less or deserve less than whites have provoked these changes.

"The result has been that on a road like the Sea Board Air Line which according to a statement made by the former Federal Manager, Mr. Harrihan, the percentage of colored locomotive firemen moved from about 5 per cent to 10 per cent for white hired largely for apprentice engineers in 1918 to "fifty-fifty." Under pay did cause a desertion of these jobs by colored men for war wages in coast industries at that time. But as late as three years ago the white organization was seeking 60 per cent of these jobs or an increase of 50 per cent in seven years. The Illinois Central is white from Cairo Junction and Mounds, Ill., on all northern and eastern divisions. On all divisions south of these points there will be found colored men in varying percentages. Instances have been reported where colored firemen with high efficiency ratings have been assigned to certain runs in order to pace the other firemen in saving fuel. On the other hand, there was recently a complaint from the Shreveport Division of the Illinois Central saying that the white firemen who now work on a "fifty-fifty" basis are asking for 60 per cent of the work. Every such shift in percentages on any road means colored men placed on the "extra board" with less employment or in the streets looking for other work.

"On the Southern Railroad and its subsidiaries, reliable informants say the percentage of colored firemen is 10 per cent or lower on some divisions. It is doubtful that it goes to 50 per cent of jobs on any division. The Louisville and Nashville has no colored firemen north of Decatur, Alabama, while south of that point the colored firemen are said to run as high as 70 per cent to 85 per cent of all men used. The hostlers jobs and the shop jobs on these roads are largely black. At the time of the Government control of the roads the Atlantic Coast Line was reputed to have 85 per cent colored firemen and engine men; the Florida East Coast 99 per cent, and the Central of Georgia almost all colored. As early as 1921 a "non-promotional" clause on the A. B. & A. Railroad was protested because Negroes suffered prospective elimination following dismissal of those then in the service. The clause allegedly read that after a certain date on following certain conditions "no man who did not stand for promotion would be hired as locomotive fireman." Negroes did not and do not stand for promotion to the grade of engineer under established American custom. Similar conditions exist on other roads where colored men fill these jobs. The Frisco stands out as determining not to employ Negroes in the future for engine and train service according to communications sent the men.

"Except in the case of the colored train porter who really does the work of a trainman when required by the conductor—and that is always—the only instances where there are differentials in pay for colored men will be found where colored men have contracted to accept lower scales of pay for self-protection. The lower rate may represent elimination of certain overtime rules or a flat rate under the so-called standard rate of the white trainmen. I believe the colored trainmen and yard switchmen of the Gulf Coast Lines with headquarters at Houston, Texas, adopted this policy. Also, the colored firemen of the same system were not agreeable to so doing according to my last information."

The Crisis, a Negro monthly reports the employment of 106 Negro trainmen on 1,100 miles of the Missouri-Pacific system.[1] These workers are members of a local union chartered by the American Federation of Labor. "They are not recognized by the white union nor are they admitted to the white union. By arrangement between the white union and the railroad, no further Negro trainmen are to be hired so that when one of the present number dies or is discharged, no other colored man takes his place."

As a further index to the problems facing Negro workers in the transportation field, is the effort of various groups to legislate

[1] Vol. 37, No. 4, Whole Number 234, April, 1930; p. 134.

Negroes out of the railway transportation occupations. Such efforts are not always obvious. Under the guise of providing a "full crew on passenger trains operating in the State of Illinois" a bill supposedly sponsored by transportation unions excluding Negro workers, was introduced into the Illinois House of Representatives by Assemblyman McCaskrin.[1] The bill stated that a minimum full train crew should consist of an engineer, a fireman, a conductor, a brakeman, and a flagman.

Negro railroad workers in Springfield, Illinois, claimed that if the bill became a law it would adversely affect hundreds of Negro train porters who were "running in charge." These workers also claimed that the bill was another effort to restrict Negro employment.

GLASS, CLAY AND STONE

Only one union of the trades organized under the head of Glass, Clay and Stone industries definitely excludes Negroes from its membership, that one being the AMERICAN FLINT GLASS WORKERS UNION. However, the small number of Negro workers under these unions' jurisdiction would in itself limit Negro membership.

The INTERNATIONAL UNION OF QUARRY WORKERS has "very few and scattering" Negro members. As the jurisdiction is not organized in the South where the majority of the six thousand Negro quarry workers are employed, the contact of this union with these workers is limited. The chief reason for Negro workers not being in the union in large numbers is due, says the International office, to "the attitude of whites who don't want us to bother *their* Negroes."

The NATIONAL WINDOW GLASS WORKERS have no Negro members because "the work seems too strenuous and does not attract them". Though the GLASS BOTTLE BLOWERS ASSOCIATION of the United States and Canada had Negro members in 1919-1920 they have none now because of the failure of their agreements with employers.

The UNITED BRICK AND CLAY WORKERS UNION with an estimated Negro membership of 100, reports on the status of Negro workers in that union as follows:

"Our experience with Negroes in the brick yards has been that they will make excellent members if educated

---

[1] Norfolk, (Va.) Journal and Guide—April 13, 1929.

to the trade union movement, and while we have a larger number of strikebreakers used against us of the colored race than we do of the white race, we do not hold that against the race as we know that it is much easier to solicit strike-breakers among the colored men in the south where they do not have an opportunity of knowing or understanding the trade union movement than it is among the white people of the north. It would be equally as easy to solicit among the white people in the south, but my experience has been that the Negro will travel where the average unintelligent white man of the south will not leave the vicinity where he has been reared.

"At the present time in the State of Connecticut, we have had a great deal of trouble with Negro strikebreakers simply because the manufacturer was smart enough to select an intelligent Negro, who for a salary was willing to lie to his own race in the south, but we have not held that against the race, but have adopted the same tactics, and have sent out intelligent Negroes from our ranks and they have very successfully broken down this movement. I venture to say that has been the means of returning not less than a thousand strikebreakers during the past year, not to mention the many thousands he kept from coming to the State of Connecticut through his visit to South Carolina, North Carolina, the Virginias and Maryland. All of us thoroughly understand the low wages paid in the South, and the Negro being in the majority among the ranks of common labor as well as the underpaid in the South is naturally the one the northern employer seeks in time of strike, and while we might go up in the air and say all sorts of things, the only real thing that can be done in the matter is to educate those that they are successful in getting in, and have our agents on the job and educate them and spread the propaganda in the south that they should not come. We have been very successful in meeting up with ministers and other leaders in the south who were fair to the labor movement and when they understood the real issue at stake would advise their friends among the colored people to remain away from the strike-bound communities.

"Among our local unions where we have Negro members who go along very well and while there is some friction at times, it does not exist any more so than among the whites themselves or among the Negroes themselves; I do not know of a single local union where local trouble ever existed during the past years that I could say originated because of the colored race.

"Outside of the Chicago District in some of our southern locals, we have a Negro membership in every local union and in some cases they are in the majority. The following illustration, I think, will prove out the success which we have had with a mixed local union—at Springfield, Ill., we have a Local No. 253, white men are in the majority, but they have a colored president who has been an officer ever since the local was organized twenty years ago. At Murphysboro where the colored men are in the majority, they have never had a colored president to my knowledge, although they have had other officials of the local and at the present time have a colored secretary and one or two minor officers. I point this out to show that as our organization is founded alone on the line of initiative, referendum and recall and if they would start any real friction that the two locals mentioned would be the exact reverse. I think that in itself speaks for harmony. We do not bar any religion, creed or color in our organization.

"There is possibly another item which might interest you when I say that we had three local unions who boasted they were 100 per cent K. K. K. during heat of that organization and I know that order existed among many of our other locals, but it did not give us a minute's worry. Instead of taking the stand that some organizations did that they would expel members who belonged to the order, we simply made a ruling through the National office to the effect that we did not care what organization they belonged to, whether it was the Odd Fellows, the K. C.'s, the Woodmen, or the K. K. K., as that was their own personal, God-given right, but if they attempted to mix any of these organizations with the Trade Union Movement to the detriment of a single member of any local union, we would expel any member who sought to do this, or if necessary would take the charter where any one local consisted of a majority. After this decision went out we did not hear a single complaint, and since it is not as big an issue as it was a few years ago, I think I can safely say that the crisis is past, although I know that the order still exists.

"In brief the only fault we have to find with the colored race is the wise, intelligent colored agents who sell their people, and you, no doubt are acquainted with these facts even more so than myself, but since they exist equally as well among the white race, that means only one thing and that is that we will have to meet the situation face to face during the campaign of education and organization, and since 'united we stand and divided we fall' has been the slogan of the Labor Movement, I am absolutely sure that we can do that better joined together than to attempt to organize as to color, creed or religion."

The NATIONAL BROTHERHOOD OF OPERATIVE POTTERS maintains that "no Negroes are employed in the organized or skilled branches in the potteries." The Minerva, Ohio, Local No. 70 is more specific in stating that Negroes are not allowed to work in the skilled pottery trades. "It is not race prejudice but custom." The Carrolton, Ohio Local No. 74 states that "we as a whole want to keep our trade white—a Negro is employed occasionally, but only until a white man is found." In Ohio many Negroes who came into the trade as strikebreakers are still in with no effort made to unionize any of them.

METALS AND MACHINERY

The unions of Blacksmiths, Boilermakers, and Machinists because of their exclusion of Negro workers have been treated in other sections of this report. The trades covered in this section, exclusive of the Electrical Workers and the Plumbers gave employment to 159,549 Negroes in 1920, approximately 130,000 of whom worked in the iron and steel industry.

THE AMALGAMATED ASSOCIATION OF IRON, STEEL AND TIN WORKERS OF NORTH AMERICA has had a most trying experience with Negro workers. This organization is the outgrowth of an amalgamation of the United Sons of Vulcan, the Associated Brotherhood of Iron and Steel Heaters, Rollers and Roughers, the Iron and Steel Roll Hands' Union, and the Nailers Union, not one of which admitted Negro members. One year before the formation of the A. A. of I. & S. Workers in 1876, Negro non-union puddlers were brought from Richmond, Virginia, to Pittsburgh, Pennsylvania, to break a strike. When the Association was formed in the following year, the preamble to its constitution stated "In union there is strength, and in the formation of a National Amalgamated Association, embracing every iron and steel worker in the country, a union founded upon a basis broad as the land in which we live, lies our only hope." Yet, no Negroes were organized.[1] The Association has not discriminated against Negroes by constitutional provision.[2] At the time of its formation white workmen in the steel industry refused to work with Negroes. Colored workers scabbed on the strikers in Pittsburgh and Homestead. Membership in the association was offered the Negro worker only after he threatened the job security of the white worker. In 1887 the union refused to declare Negro members eligible, but in 1881 they were permitted to join, "past experience having taught the craft that they were indispensable." As a result Negro workers were organized wherever possible. Separate locals were found in Pittsburgh in 1887 and later in several southern cities. That, however, was little protection as white workmen in Birmingham, Alabama, refused to work with Negroes even after they became eligible for membership.[3] The relationship of Negroes with this union has not been very satisfactory. Its passive activity during the great steel strike was classed by Wm. Z. Foster as "treason to the whole labor movement."[4]

In 1928 there were approximately 300 Negro workers in this union. A part of the obligation given to the members of the A. A. of I. S. and T. W. of North America upon joining the organization is:

"First, the general improvement of all members of our craft, socially, morally, mentally and financially; Second, to cultivate and promote feelings of sympathy, love and friendship among all members and obliterate all line of demarcation, caused by creed or nationality."

The International Lodge admits that it has not had much success in organizing Negroes, because "the boss tells the Negro that if he joins the union he will hire white men and vice versa".

Despite the fact that the laws permit Negro membership, Mayfair Lodge No. 25 of Chicago "will not vote to accept their applications for social reasons". The Cleveland Lodge has no Negro members, though they are not barred, and despite the fact that there are more than 3,000 Negro workers in iron and steel

[1] Wright, R. R. Jr., The Negro in Pennsylvania, pp. 94-100.
[2] Robinson, Jesse S., The Amalgamated Association of Iron, Steel and Tin Workers.
[3] Ibid.
[4] Foster, Wm. Z. The Great Steel Strike and Its Lesson.

in that city. In Cannonsburg, Pa., Lodge No. 79 has 18 Negro members representing 100 per cent organization. There "is no discrimination of any kind whatsoever' and so far as that lodge is concerned, "we wish that all Negroes were as good union men as those that we have." The Blue Valley Lodge No. 2 of Kansas City, Mo., "tolerates Negroes but does not urge them to join". Furthermore, Negro workers can "get by without joining". If they do come into the union they "feel whites don't want them". Six Negroes are members of Trumbull Lodge No. 73 of Warren, Ohio and the local admits that "the old prejudices intervene to keep the boys from some jobs". The Lebanon, Pennsylvania Lodge No. 91 believes that Negroes are "afraid of their jobs". Though there are no Negroes in the union at present, the few that were members were "dropped"; the Negro strikebreakers who formerly worked there "left town"; and the non-union men "never did join". In Warren, Ohio, Negro workers were organized by Local No. 78 around 1920 but they did not "stick." Officials of this union believe that Negro workers are "not steady" workers or union members. Because of the problems of organization the corresponding representative says "of course we have to take them in if they make application—but we are making no efforts to get them."

Lodges of iron and steel workers are located in Newport and Louisville, Ky., and a few other southern cities.

John Fitch in his study "The Steel Workers"[1] shows that the Association "has always been an organization of skilled workers and has centered its efforts on securing better conditions for that class of labor alone". Mr. Fitch also found that one of the problems of the Association was "the clannishness of the races making up its original membership. These included Scotch, Irish, Welsh, English, and Americans, and there seems to have been a good deal of race antagonism."

THE INTERNATIONAL MOLDERS' UNION has often seen the shadow of black labor darken its prospects for success. The early problems faced by the union are summed up as follows.[2]

Negroes were first employed in foundries as laborers. In the course of time they proved able to pick up parts of the molding trade, chiefly in stove, sashweight and pipe shops. White molders, who disliked the competition of the colored

---

[1] Pages 97-98.

[2] Vide. Stockton, International Molders Union of North America, p. 59.

"handy man" and association with him, endeavored to stop his progress in the trade by ridiculing his clumsy efforts and his inferior results. Finally, however, the Negro's willingness to accept extremely low wages began to cause alarm. Notwithstanding this danger to their scales, the local unions in the South, for racial reasons entirely, excluded Negroes from membership through the unwillingness of their members to propose a Negro's name. By 1896 the competition of Negro molders had become so acute that the executive board, moved in part by complaints from employers of white labor, condemned the "racial prejudice of a past generation" and strongly urged that efforts be made to organize the Negroes of the South and thus counteract their "debasing influence" upon the trade.[1] To carry out this plan proved a difficult problem because the Negro had not forgotten "the bitter antagonism with which his original aspirations were confronted" and because he feared that preference would be granted the white molder if he demanded equal pay for equal work.[2] The situation was further complicated when several local unions, both in the "border states" and in the "far South", flatly refused to admit Negro molders. In 1900 the international officers definitely took charge of the situation. At their solicitation Local No. 53, of Chattanooga, where the Negro molder predominated, agreed to make an effort to organize colored journeymen. A few of the latter took out cards, but they quickly dropped their membership when their employers threatened to make affiliation with unions a cause for discharge. Since it proved difficult to get Chattanooga Negroes into a regular local union a "protectorate" was established over the district through an independent colored local union which paid no dues to the International and which, in fact, was under no obligations of any sort to that body. The latter, however, promised financial assistance to the Negro union and stipulated that no white molder would be allowed to take the place of a colored journeyman on strike. The new plan did not work satisfactorily since the Negroes seemed to feel that with their inferior skill they were better off out of labor organizations than in them.[3]

John P. Frey, Secretary of the Metal Trades Department of the American Federation of Labor reports the Chattanooga difficulty as follows:

[1] Iron Molders' Journal, July, 1896, p. 279.
[2] Ibid., July, 1898, p. 328.
[3] The case mentioned here is the only instance where the Molders have ever formed a local union independent of the central body.

"In Chattanooga at the time that I organized the first union of colored molders which was ever organized, there were about 350 or 400 white molders working in the city, and there were about the same number of Negro molders. In a few of the foundries they were what is called "mixed". They both worked under the same roof, but with Negroes on one side and whites on the other. In some of the foundries they were all white and in some of the others they were all colored.

"First of all I had to convince the members of my own union that the question was not a social one, that it was purely an economic one, that a casting made by a Negro molder was just as good as a casting made by a white molder—and although they did everything but throw me out of the meeting room—finally they yielded.

"When I talked with the leaders of the Negro molders I found them intelligent men—willing to be pioneers.

"About six months after the organization of this local union, I received a letter from the officers telling me that a special meeting had been called, and that I must be present. The president ——— said that he hoped I would not misunderstand their position, but that they had finally reached the conclusion that it was not feasible for them to have a union. He said: "the foundrymen have told us that they do not want any union, and if we keep on they are going to discharge some of us; and if we are discharged how are we going to work as molders any other place in the South? If we remain active in the union we will lose our positions, and then besides, we think that you white molders are always going to fight for higher wages and shorter hours, and when you do get shorter hours, then the foundrymen will have to give us a little more to keep us from organizing.

"And so they surrendered their local union for the reasons they gave."[1]

For several years the general situation remained unchanged, except that the number of Negro molders increased. The international officers steadily carried on a campaign of education

[1] Frey, John P., Attempts to Organize Negro Workers. The American Federationist, March, 1929, Vol. 36, No. 3, pp. 296-305.

designed to show the necessity of recognizing the Negro. Members contended that the admission of Negroes would induce more of them to enter the trade, but the officers pointed out that the union had to deal with a condition, not a theory, since there were already seven or eight hundred Negroes employed at molding. The members were asked whether they desired to make the Negro an ally or a permanent non-unionist, whose employment would prevent the organization from obtaining control of many important shops. In 1911 the view of the International finally gained recognition. In that year the Birmingham local union, the largest in the South, not only decided to admit all Negro molders and coremakers in its jurisdiction, but it also made vigorous efforts to carry out its policy. Since 1911 other local unions have also let down the bars. The actual organization of Negroes, however, has proceeded slowly.

Because the organization keeps no record of Negro membership, it is impossible to give an estimate. Returns from eleven locals with 3,360 members showed 12 Negroes. The organization of Negroes has met with "very poor success" because of "intimidation on the part of the employer, and indifference on the part of the Negro.[1] A special privilege is given Negroes permitting them to "have separate local unions with all rights and privileges of the whites."

The one Negro molder belonging to Local No. 176 of Minneapolis was suspended. In Alliance, Ohio "they are not given a chance to learn the trade". In Cincinnati, there are no Negroes in Locals No. 3 or No. 4, but the Financial Secretary of Local No. 3 states that there are about 150 Negroes working in unfair shops who should be organized. The suggestion is made that these workers organize and stay in one shop and "not allow white men to work in it. This would be an advantage to both white and Negro molders." There are 12 Negro molders in Unions Nos. 27,218, and 430 of Cleveland. Those that are members are "good, staunch ones", and their relation with white members is "unbiased". The Cleveland situation is explained in more detail as follows:

"During the strikes here in 1916 and 1917 Negroes were imported from the South and their minds were poisoned against organized labor before they reached here. They were employed under camouflaged conditions.

---

[1] Statement of M. J. Keough, President I. M. U. of N. A.

"They were transported to and from their place of employment by automobiles and were not permitted to talk or listen to strikers or their representatives under penalty of discharge. Their transportation was deducted from their earnings.

"We have no fear of the Negro strikebreakers as molders. Foundrymen get no results from them since they don't produce castings that can be sold. They are used mostly to discourage the strikers. When strikes are over they are replaced regardless which side won.

"We have taken many Negroes in our organization only to find out they misrepresented themselves and could not hold a job.

"The days of discrimination against the Negro in our organization have passed."

Despite the fact that the SHEET METAL WORKERS NATIONAL ASSOCIATION at its St. Paul Convention, gave to colored workers the right to establish their own unions, there were no colored locals affiliated with the Association in 1927. The racial identity of members is not revealed by the records. There are, however, no Negro members of the S. M. W. N. A. in the South, and only seven were located in the North, four of whom were in New York City.

In Savannah, Georgia, and in Charleston, S. C., there are separate Negro unions of Sheet Metal Workers not affiliated with the Association. According to Wm. L. Sullivan, Secretary of this Union—"They have different working conditions from those under which the white union men in the same trade and in the same city work. The colored workers work nine hours and the white workers eight hours. Thus the unions of colored men have little or no economic value. And the Sheet Metal Workers Association having no jurisdiction over the colored locals is not in a position to effect standard wages and working conditions. The chief benefits of these Negro locals are fraternal ones."

No Negroes were located in the INTERNATIONAL UNION OF METAL POLISHERS. Local No. 3 of Cleveland, Ohio, had a few "some years ago" but they became unfinancial and were dropped.

There were only 46 Negro pattern and mold workers in the United States in 1920 and none of these was affiliated with the PATTERN MAKERS ASSOCIATION.

THE STOVE MOUNTERS' INTERNATIONAL ASSOCIATION has no Negro members.

The UNITED AUTOMOBILE, AIRCRAFT AND VEHICLE WORKERS Local, No. 49, New York, has 50 Negro members. Negroes drop out of this union because of lack of work.

The ARCHITECTURAL IRON, BRONZE AND STRUCTURAL WORKERS UNION OF NEW YORK, while not reporting the number of members reports that Negroes "are gradually joining"

THE AMALGAMATED METAL WORKERS OF AMERICA [1] not affiliated to the American Federation of Labor, reports 4,000 members of whom 12 are Negroes. In New York, membership is open to "all wage workers in the metal, machine and allied industries regardless of creed, color, or sex."

The INTERNATIONAL BROTHERHOOD OF FOUNDRY EMPLOYEES reports 150 Negro members. In this union the successful handling of a strike by International officers created very friendly relations between the white and Negro members.

MINING, OIL AND LUMBER

None of the unions whose jurisdiction is found in the field of mining, oil and lumber prohibits Negro membership. The INTERNATIONAL UNION OF MINE, MILL AND SMELTER WORKERS admits no individual holding membership in the I. W. W. or in any union not recognized by the American Federation of Labor. It is composed of workers in the mill mining industry, covering specifically miners, smeltermen, millmen and refining and blast furnace workers. Approximately 500 Negroes were members of the union in 1926. In 1927, however, Negroes were "very few and scattering". In the previous year there were three locals of Negro workers at Mulberry, Florida, but between 1926 and 1927 all of the Negro membership in the southern states, except Arkansas was lost. The union correspondent was unable to state "why we lost these locals."

The UNITED MINE WORKERS OF AMERICA has been one of the outstanding unions with Negro membership. Though the Negro membership in 1927 is no more than 5,000, as late as 1920, 25,000 Negro miners were said to be affiliated to the organization. During the coal strike of 1922, Negroes were imported

---

[1] This independent group has died out since the investigation was started.

from the southern states to the Western Pennsylvania coal field. The United Mine Workers delegated an organizer to meet the newcomers for the purpose of informing them of the controversy between the union and the operators. As a result the locals in Western Pennsylvania gained as members hundreds of Negroes who had been imported to promote the strike.

During the middle 90's the United Mine Workers spent much of its organized efforts in the fields of McDowell and Fayette Counties in West Virginia. This policy succeeded in organizing more than almost half of Fayette County and three-fourths of McDowell County. The men who were leading the organization of McDowell County seemed to have received bribes to discontinue their activity. They left the state and the union movement died aborning. It is said that one Negro miner loaned the United Mine Workers fifteen thousand dollars to aid the organization of the county. According to the record, he never received a cent of his money back and in the last five years of his life was supported by the coal company for which he was working when the strike began.[1]

In Logan County, West Virginia, where approximately one-third of the miners were Negroes and mines had not been organized, and when in 1921 the efforts of the United Mine Workers to organize this field failed, the union was literally wrecked. When the armed march of miners from Kanawha and Fayette Counties into Mingo County was effected in 1921, there were a large number of Negroes in the group. At the same time there were two Negro members on the Executive Board of the United Mine Workers, District No. 15.

When the bituminous fields of Western Pennsylvania were recruiting a new labor force during the coal strike of 1927, the Negro miner was most in demand. In 1924 one company had 586 Negroes in its employ who formed 5 per cent of its total work force. In 1927 the same company employed 3,704 Negro workers who represented 41 per cent of the total employees. Another company employing 2,000 workers had 800 Negroes.[2]

According to A. W. Johnson, a Negro miner and secretary of the Local Union No. 2950, U. M. W. of A., who has mined for

---

[1] Harris, A. L., The Negro in the Coal Mining Industry—Opportunity, Journal of Negro Life. Vol. 4, No. 2—February, 1926.

[2] The Coal Strike in Western Pennsylvania, Federal Council of Churches, p. 66.

thirty-three years and has been a member of the U. M. W. of A. for twenty-one years, "Huge gangs of Negro workers were inveigled from the South, ignorant of the fact that there was a desperate struggle between the union miners and the coal companies." Johnson further maintains that "the United Mine Workers of America have done more to remove hatred and prejudice in the labor movement and to restore harmony and good will between man and man than any other agency in the country.[1]

In the southern fields where the Negro worker forms a larger percentage of the total miners, the policy of organization has been almost ignored. It is in the vicinities of Ohio, Pennsylvania and Illinois that the chief activity of the United Mine Workers has brought forth union and members. In Bellair, Ohio, the American Negro Labor Congress brought into the organization 16 Negro members that had not previously belonged in other towns in Ohio. The importation of Negro miners as strikebreakers has resulted in the establishment of towns in which there are no Negro persons; in other towns there are no white persons. Local 1256 in Columbus, Ohio, reported 75 out of 270. Local 2057 at Whitsett, Pennsylvania, had an agreement with the Pittsburgh Coal Company which was repudiated on August 20, 1925. At that time there were three colored members of this local one of whom was vice-president and the other financial secretary and check weighman. Two of these men returned to work as "scabs" while the other remained out until the union was completely whipped.

When in 1925 the United Mine Workers was engaged in a strike in the Western Pennsylvania coal fields, an organizer of the union wrote as follows: "We have a strike on at this time with the Pittsburgh Coal Company and three-fourths of the men working as strikebreakers are Negroes—and bad ones too. They were the first to enter mines. The Pittsburgh Coal Company signed an agreement with the United Mine Workers and this agreement should not expire until April 1, 1927, yet this company has broken the Jacksonville agreement and has tried to work the mines on the non-union basis. They are bringing colored men here to take the place of men who are resisting the thing the coal company is trying to do. We have some white scum also, but the Negro is in the majority."

The NATIONAL MINERS UNION was organized as a "left wing" organization following the collapse of the United Mine Workers

---

[1] Pittsburgh (Pa.) Courier—February, 1928.

in Western Pennsylvania, Illinois and the Northern West Virginia coal fields. The extent of Negro membership in this organization is not known, though it has been particularly active among Negro miners in the Northern West Virginia fields. A Negro, who was formerly a district official of the United Mine Workers Union, is national Vice President of this organization.

Neither the LOYAL LEGION OF LOGGERS AND LUMBERMEN nor the INTERNATIONAL ASSOCIATION OF OIL FIELD, GAS WELL AND REFINERY WORKERS reported on the number of Negro members.

CLOTHING AND TEXTILES

BOOT AND SHOE WORKERS UNION. This organization admits to membership any male or female boot and shoe worker over sixteen years of age. When the Knights of St. Crispin became affiliated with the Knights of Labor, Negroes and women were admitted to membership on the same basis as white male members. The number of Negroes in the trade, however, has been small. While there are approximately 50 Negroes in the union in New York, replies from other sections of the country show their membership in that trade to be negligible. In Milwaukee, Wisconsin, only one Negro is employed as a shoe cutter. In Philadelphia, Pennsylvania, 4 Negroes are members of the Boot and Shoe Workers Union No. 384. The Philadelphia organization has made efforts to get Negro membership, but it has had practically no success. The Philadelphia Trades and Labor Council and the A. N. L. C. have given aid in the organization of Negro worker. In Cincinnati, Ohio, there are no Negroes employed in the shoe industry. St. Paul, Minnesota, reports no Negro members.

The AMALGAMATED CLOTHING WORKERS OF AMERICA gives no figures but reports through Joseph R. Scholossberg, the general secretary and treasurer: "There are very few Negroes in the organization because there are very few in the industry.

The INTERNATIONAL FUR WORKERS UNION OF THE UNITED STATES AND CANADA reports that there are no Negroes in the fur industry. An analysis of the returns from individual locals however, shows that there is no discrimination as to creed or color in the industry. The union reports a membership of 1,200. In New York City there are 10 organized Negro workers, and St. Paul, Minnesota, reports one. The New York joint board reports that the Negro workers in the fur industry are "all right". They are chiefly the semi-skilled workers in the industry. Two

Negro men were quite active in Local No. 10 of this organization. One of them played a very prominent part in the recent strike held in the city. Incidentally, the race problems in the fur industry is not centered around the Negro, but around the Greek, who, it is claimed, "scabs all the time". The secretary of the joint board claimed that "Nigger workers" were all right, —that there were a number of "girl niggers" in the unorganized shops, and at one time a "girl nigger" was president of the local fur workers union.

THE INTERNATIONAL LADIES GARMENT WORKERS UNION keeps no record of its membership by race or color. When, however, a recent strike in the New York shops disclosed the fact that there were approximately 4,000 Negro women employed in the 3,500 dress shops of the city, of whom no more than 200 were members of the International Ladies Garment Workers, this union started an organization effort among Negro clothing workers. A Negro organizer was employed for the purpose. In this study 519 Negro members were found in twelve locals of this organization. In Local No. 50, of Philadelphia there have been Negro members since 1916. There was no extensive organization among colored women and girls until 1921. In 1925 the union employed a colored organizer who through house to house canvass and personal contacts outside of the shops brought in more than one hundred colored women.

In April 1926 there was a strike of this local in a shop which involved white unionists and colored non-trade unionists. The colored workers declined to join with the white unionists because they planned to be in the trade only a short time. One woman was working only to help her husband establish himself as a pharmacist; another had her family to care for, hence, "she could not afford to quit work"; another colored woman secured nine strikebreakers for the shop. In this strike the union lost, but the colored strikebreakers did not keep their jobs.

In many other instances, however, the local has received considerable support from colored women and girls in the shops, particularly where whites were in the majority. There are approximately 1,000 colored women and girls employed in the garment industry in Philadelphia.

In New York there have been many problems of organization. Negro workers are used chiefly as pressers, finishers and cleaners. The executive of one union reports that (1) colored workers are not inclined to train for the advanced lines, they are content in following the less skilled occupations; (2) these Negro workers shift to domestic work when facing unemployment; (3) the white worker takes domestic employment as a last resort and sticks to the trade for advancement; (4) the colored girl is unsteady, lacks appreciation of trade lines; (5) Negroes are not informed on trade unionism and employers take advantage of this fact to make colored workers feel their incompetency. When strikes are called the Negro is not interested because of his failure to understand trade union principles. Two Negro workers, however, are on the executive board of Local No. 22.

According to Julius Hochman, Vice President of the I. L. G. W. Union, one of the features of the present time is a special campaign to organize all of the colored workers employed in the dress industry. A special department of the international has been established for this purpose. The difficulties facing such an organization scheme are recited as follows.[1]

"At the meeting called for Tuesday, September 26 (1929) at St. Luke's Hall, a group of colored 'organizers' on the payroll of the Communist Party, broke into the meeting and began to make their usual accusations that our union is opposed to the colored belonging, that the rights of the colored people are not protected, that the colored people's only hope is the Communist Party. One by one the girls who attended the meeting, a large number who have been members of the union rose and from their own experiences told of the absolute equality of membership in our union, of how their interests were protected, how the union in many instances called strikes to force the employers to give them the same privileges, pay them the same wages, and treat them the same as all other union people, and unanimously ordered the Communist disrupters out of the meeting."

The present organization plan appears encouraging, and, according to Floria Pinckney, the Negro woman selected as organizer, the union hopes to have 600 new Negro members by April, 1930. In this campaign the I. L. G. W. Union is enlisting the aid of colored organizations and individuals who are in sympathy with the "American organized labor movement".

The constitution of the UNITED GARMENT WORKERS OF AMERICA provides "you also promise—never to discriminate—on

---

[1] Hochman, Julius, Organizing the Dressmakers. The American Federationist, December, 1929. Volume 36, No. 12—Page 1466.

account of creed, color or nationality." The number of Negro workers in the union is small. The general secretary reports that "our experience has been that the Negro is a loyal trade unionist when organized. There are several of our cutters local unions who have colored cutters in the north. Of course this could not happen in the south. We had a local of colored women at one time but for some unknown reason it disbanded, but we felt the women were good trade unionists. There were a few among them who were not willing to work, but I find that among our white locals also. But taking it all in all, I look with favor upon an organization of Negro labor affiliated to the American Federation of Labor".

New York reports approximately 100 Negro members, while the Chicago District Council estimates its Negro membership at 30[1] In Cincinnati, no Negro has ever made application for membership, while in Erie, Pennsylvania, Local No. 930 never having had an application, would organize Negroes if "there were enough to form a union of their own and they were not forced to mingle with the white girls, they would be welcomed in the labor field".

The INTERNATIONAL UNION OF GLOVE WORKERS reports only 2 Negro members. The secretary of this union reports "that the question of Negro membership came up in the local on the Pacific coast. The policy of the American Federation of Labor was stated and a firm stand taken by the secretary of the international with the result that a favorable decision was given".

The INTERNATIONAL UNION OF CLOTH HAT, CAP AND MILLINERY WORKERS reports a Negro membership of 300, located chiefly in New York City. They are reputed to be as good members as are the whites, and were not important factors in a strike held in 1919. Their status in the union "is exactly the same as that of our white members".

The UNITED HATTERS OF NORTH AMERICA. No Negro members are reported by this organization. It appears that the Negroes working in this industry are employed chiefly in the non-union shops, or in the unskilled position of union shops. Even in the unorganized shops in the vicinity of Danbury and Norwalk, Connecticut, Negro workers are employed on the unskilled and semi-skilled operations.

---

[1] Subsequent reports estimate the Negro membership as 275.

The UNITED NECKWEAR WORKERS. No. 6939 is affiliated directly to the American Federation of Labor. The business representative of this union knows of no Negroes engaged in the trade.

The JOURNEYMEN TAILORS' UNION OF AMERICA is of the opinion that there are very few Negro tailors who can make a coat, vest and pants, and for that reason there are few of them in the union. Eight locals of this organization reported a total Negro membership of 17.

The INTERNATIONAL UNION OF LEATHER WORKERS. Eight Negro members were reported as belonging to this union in 1927. Before the war there were a number of Negro members who were forced to leave the organization along with several hundred white workers when the industrial depression depleted its ranks. In New York City, the Trade Union Committee for Organizing Negro Workers assisted the union in promoting a strike in which four Negro workers were involved as strikebreakers.

TEXTILES

(Because of the current interest in Southern textile mills and because of the recent organization efforts in that industry, a preface on employment of Negroes in Southern mills is added to this section.)

Two hundred and sixty thousand of the 460,000 cotton textile workers in the United States are in the Southern States of Alabama, Georgia, North Carolina, South Carolina, Tennessee and Virginia.

But the work that these mills offer is for white workers. Such has been the case since the day of William Gregg. Coming out of the Civil War socially and economically disorganized, the white workers faced the competition of the Negro ex-slaves. The cotton manufacturers felt a moral compulsion in their business and accompanied the development of mill sites with what Dr. Broadus Mitchell has chosen to call "a desire to give employment to the necessitous masses of the poor whites, for the sake of the people themselves." Such a purpose has persisted in the minds of Southern manufacturers and mill operatives. The institution stands as another of the many examples of the racial hierarchy of American industry. The Negro was permitted employment in the planting, tending, and picking the staple product, ginning, storing, trucking at the mill, cleaning the mill yards, firing, and all processes up to and including "picking", one of the least skilled and least remunerative of all the mill operations. There, however, his chances ended. All mills were not so generous in their employment policies. One mill secured the cooperation of the municipality wherein it was located, and had its legislative body pass a law prohibiting any Negro from ever working therein.

The persistence of such an exclusion policy, however, has not been a logical one. Attempts were made to discredit the ability of the Negro to do this type of work. Marjorie Potwin[1] points out in her study that the Negro was less conspicuous in the textile industry than in any other phase of Southern life. In the experimental stage of the industry in the Piedmont section, Negro workers were assigned to such jobs as scrubbing, firing the boilers, driving mules, etc. Three or four experiments were attempted in elevating the Negro to the rank of textile operatives. Incidentally, they all failed, the reasons given ranging from estimates of the economic effect on his temperament and his slow muscle reaction to social explanations on the undesirability of racial admixture. Negro masons put up the walls of the mills, and Negro labor built the roads, but when the mills were ready to operate only Negro firemen, coal rollers and two or three scrub women were permitted to work therein.

The ability of the Negro to perform the operations in cotton manufacturing is seen in evidence from the days prior to the Civil War when factories were rare. The Saluda factory, near Columbia, S. C. serves as example of the proficiency of these workers. Though manned by slaves, the superintendent found that they could endure the work of the cotton factories better than the whites. This mill employed 128 operatives, the overseers and superintendent being the only white persons used. It consisted of 5,000 spindles and 120 looms, and manufactured shirting and a coarse kind of colored goods. At first these workers were used in the shipping department, and gradually shifted to the weaving rooms. According to the head weaver the Negroes did just as much work as the white workers and were far more attentive to the looms. Two years of experimentation followed and slave operatives were found more satisfactory than the white workers and at a 30 per cent saving in labor costs. Ironically, at the close of the Civil War this labor was replaced by white workers.

[1] Potwin, Marjorie—Cotton Mill People in the Piedmont, A Study in social change, 1927.

Other mills in Florida, Alabama and South Carolina used Negro labor. In fact so successful were the many experiments that in 1850 and 1851 at the conventions of cotton planters held in Montgomery, Alabama, and Macon, Georgia, respectively; resolutions were introduced urging the creation of cotton mills in every county of the cotton growing states. The conventions further resolved, that Negro slaves were well able to attend to the looms, and were the "best and cheapest labor" in the world.

It appears that the slave economy was the only reason for the employment of Negro workers. Since that time the criticism has been that the Negro of today is less reliable than his progenitors. The truth of the situation, however, lay in the competition white workers were suffering with the employment of Negroes. Certain mills, after 1870 used Negro help exclusively and set up in the small towns a feudalism for Negroes that was as ignoble as that of the average white mill village. In the main there was an existing fear that Negroes would be unreliable and unprofitable as free men. To this end, the South Carolina legislators passed an act for the encouragement of European emigration, while Alabama incorporated the German Immigration Society, and Georgia, Arkansas and Texas made organized efforts to secure foreign workers. Chinese workers "undesirable to neither white nor black" were also considered. But their efforts met with little success and the exigencies of the period enabled white workers to enter the mills in large numbers. For a time Negro and white workers were employed on similar operations in the same room. Not all of these were successful however, and the unsuccessful experiments were loudly heralded and often illogically interpreted. The conclusion reached by the management of one mill where Negro labor was used, was to the effect that such labor should never be employed in mills located near natural bodies of water. Because fish is the thing dearest to the Negro's heart—(watermelon excepted) —Negro workers in this mill, it is claimed, would quit at midday and spend their afternoons fishing, refusing to work at any price. On the other hand, Negro girls proved their efficiency as mill operatives in La Grange, Georgia, where they excelled the whites.

Negroes are excluded because of their inefficiency, but it is interesting to note that the success with native white labor has not been the most satisfactory. A government report on the subject in 1923 states that "turnover and movement of these workers shows unrest and dissatisfaction with the conditions." This probably is expected from the property-less whites who are used in large numbers, the group described by Kephart[1] as—

"—deluded by what seems easy money, they sell their little homesteads for just enough cash to set them up as workers in town.—Being untrained in any trade, they can only get the lowest wages which are quickly dissipated in rents and in food that formerly they raised for themselves. Unused to continuous labor, they irk under its discipline, drop out, and fall into desultory habits."

Within the last twenty years, however, there have been gross changes in the employment of Negro labor. While they do not bespeak a preponderance of Negroes in the industry, they point to a greater use of them as the industry expands, and as labor demands become more pressing. Negro textile workers increased from 2,949 in 1900, to 24,794 in 1920. The increase is shown more formidably by the 13,401 Negro workers who were added to the industry between 1910 and 1920. These workers were distributed as follows:

TABLE VIII
Distribution of Negro Workers in Textile Industries
1910-1920

| | BY SEX | | | |
| | 1910 | | 1920 | |
	MALE	FEMALE	MALE	FEMALE
Carpet Mills	252	27	165	105
Cotton Mills	6,333	883	12,782	3,733
Hemp and Jute	212	9	180	9
Knitting	542	274	643	1,348
Lace and Embroidery	29	136	52	210
Linens	21	18	14	25
Rope and Cordage	228	34	682	91
Sails. Tents and Awnings	62	5	131	13
Silks	187	373	292	313
Textile Dyeing	536	109	699	137
Woolen & Worsted Mills	277	66	460	201
Not specified	420	300	1,437	1,072
Total	9,099	2,234	17,537	7,257

[1] Our Southern Highlanders, Kephart.

The type of work that the Negroes do, however, is distinctly pictured by the fact that though there are approximately four semi-skilled operatives to one laborer in the cotton industry, among the Negro workers there is approximately one semi-skilled employee to every eight laborers. At the same time 3,649 or 22.1 per cent of all the Negro workers are semi-skilled, that number exceeding the total semi-skilled Negroes in the chemical and allied industries, as well as the clay, glass and stone manufactories.

The geographical distribution of the Negro workers shows that 66.3 per cent of the total Negro employees in cotton mills in 1920 were in the states of Georgia, Alabama, North Carolina and South Carolina. These same states provide 61.3 per cent of the total Negro textile employees.

TABLE IX

Distribution of Total and Negro Employees in Textile Mills and in Cotton Mills for Selected States—1920

	Total Negro Employees in All Textile Mills	Total Negro Employees in Cotton Mills	Unskilled	Semi-Skilled
Georgia	4,642	4.450	3,873	577
North Carolina	4,172	2,817	2,506	311
Alabama	3,272	2,270	1,852	418
South Carolina	3.077	3,075	2,765	310
Massachusetts	1,918	1.188	123	1,065

Coexistant with the underemployment of Negro workers is the low wage paid them. Despite the general low wage scale for all workers in the industry, that for Negro workers is lower even when performing the same operations. This fact has been repeatedly brought out by the reports of the Women's Bureau of the Department of Labor in its studies. That Bureau in 1921 made a study of 39 textile establishments in Alabama employing 3,485 women of whom 246 or 12.1 per cent were Negroes. There were 212 Negro women employed in cotton industries. The median weekly wage for these workers was $5.50 as compared with $9.50 for white women. Thirty per cent of the Negro women and 43 per cent of the white women had more than five years experience in the industry. During the same year in Georgia, of 245 Negro women employed in the textile mills, 190 worked on a time payment basis, 50 on piece work, and 5 on both. Tennessee cotton mills in 1924 paid a median weekly wage of $10.80 to white women and $7.60 to Negroes.

It was hoped in some quarters, however, that the rapid expansion of these mills in southern states would effect a change, while others saw no opportunity for the Negro workers. An economist and special writer for one of the financial weeklies states the existing situation as follows.[1]

"Last December, when I was investigating mill conditions in New England, Mr. E. Howard Bennett of the *American Wool and Cotton Reporter,* told me that when white labor becomes scarce in the South the mills will fall back on Negro labor, using all Negroes in these departments in which any are used; in other words not mixing the two races in any department. He offered to prove the prognostication, and endeavored to do so by the claim, which is perfectly true, that mill work is easy enough for anybody to learn . . . On my trip South this summer, I inquired along this line. Without going too much into detail, I came to the conclusion that practically no Southern mill men, if indeed any, have the slightest thought of using Negro labor in their mills beyond the picker room. In the first place, they don't need to, in this generation at least. In the second place, while Negroes could learn the work, and could actually do it—they require too constant supervision to make good mill workers. Their tendency to soldier on a job where they are not constantly watched is well known, especially in the south.

"I do not believe there is any likelihood that we shall ever see cotton mills run by Negroes, although the gradual infusion of white blood and a process of selection of the fittest by a few mills may one day lead to their being used here and there in coarse good mills."

MacDonald and Thompson in more recent studies of Southern mill areas hold similar views. The latter writer maintaining that there is no general disposition toward the use of Negro labor because of; (1) the feeling that Negroes are incapable as machine tenders; (2) the social question of relationship between white and black workers; (3) a sufficient supply of cheap white labor. At

---

[1] Vide: Opportunity. Journal of Negro Life. Vol. 4. No. 39, p. 96. March, 1926.

that time Negro workers were known to be employed in mills located in Durham, North Carolina; Lynchburg, Virgina; and possibly several other cities.[1]

Labor organization in textile manufacturing is industrial in character with craft divisions, the general organization being the central federation of craft unions within the industry. The UNITED TEXTILE WORKERS OF AMERICA is the largest of these unions, and on January 27, 1926, President Thomas M. McMahon reported no Negro members. The constitution of this organization does not prevent Negroes from joining. In fact, "the white workers of the south were the first to suggest that we give a charter to the Negroes. This took place a few years ago in the city of Columbus, Georgia, and a year later another charter was issued in Concord, N. C. on the suggestion of white workers." Negroes and whites are admitted on the same terms but in different locals. Negroes drop out of the unions, however, because the dues are thought to be too high. In commenting upon the relationship between Negroes and whites in the textile industry, the following facts are given. "(Q) Do you regard the organization of Negroes as essential to the success of the labor movement? (A) Yes, these people are doing all the dirty and laborious work in the mills of the South. (Q) Please comment on the relations of white and Negro members of your organization. (A) In so far as I know the whites *use* Negroes well and get along fine." According to Paul Blanshard, the local unions of Negro workers formed by the U. T. W. were in centers where there were strong white unions. The formation of these locals gave critics a chance to inject the race issue. White workers became uneasy and the most prosperous of these unions did not last over two years.

THE NATIONAL TEXTILE WORKERS UNION, sponsored by Communist organizations, is the union that first agitated the recent unionization of textile workers in the South. It has attempted, and with partial success, the organization of Negro and white workers into the same unions. The membership of the National Textile Workers has been built from disaffected groups of the older textile unions and new workers heretofore unreached.

The AMERICAN FEDERATION OF TEXTILE OPERATIVES is composed of 16 local unions distributed in the New England states. The Negro membership was not obtainable.

---

[1] Vide: MacDonald, Lois—Southern Mill Hills, p. 18.
Thompson—From Cotton Field to Cotton Mill, pp. 248-268.

THE AMALGAMATED LACE OPERATORS report that the lace industry came from Great Britain and "to the best of our knowledge we have never had a Negro in our ranks."

PAPER, PRINTING AND BOOKBINDING

The INTERNATIONAL BROTHERHOOD OF PAPER MAKERS. Only 2 Negroes are known to be members of this union. According to the international president "There is no special reason for this that I know of other than the fact that our membership is made up mostly of skilled workers and the colored man has not sought employment at our trade. As a matter of fact, I know positively of only one colored man who is a member of our organization. This man is employed at Fort Francis, Ontario, having formerly worked at Berlin, N. H. He has been in the trade for years and is a splendid fellow and is accorded all the privileges and benefits of any other member of the organization. He is one of the highest skilled in our industry."

THE INTERNATIONAL BROTHERHOOD OF PULP, SULPHITE AND PAPER MILL WORKERS admits Negroes to membership if they are employed in the trade jurisdiction. In 1926, however, there was only one Negro member in the total membership of 10,000. With the development of the industry in the South, it is found that there are more Negroes coming into the trade organization. A few years ago there was a very large organization at Canton, N. C. with a large Negro membership. When a strike was held in that locality and lost, the union was destroyed. The president of this union states "it is difficult to organize both black and white workers. Why the Negro does not join the union and remain a member is beyond me. The same applies to the white workers."

The UNITED WALL PAPER CRAFTS OF NORTH AMERICA draws no line against color or creed. The international union reports that there are no Negro wall paper printers, color mixers.

The INTERNATIONAL PLATE PRINTERS, DIE STAMPERS AND ENGRAVERS UNION OF NORTH AMERICA reports that "we have no Negroes employed at our trade".

The INTERNATIONAL PHOTO ENGRAVERS UNION reports, through replies received from unions covering 5,393 of its 8,300 members, only 2 Negroes—one in Philadelphia and one in New York. The Philadelphia member "works shoulder to shoulder" with his fellow trade unionists with no feeling whatsoever. The relationship between the Negro worker in New York and his white associates is described as "very good". Local No. 4 in Buffalo, N. Y. does not believe it advisable to seek any Negro workers, while Union No. 2 of Baltimore knows of no reason other than the usual prejudice against the Negro that makes his membership undesirable.

The AMALGAMATED LITHOGRAPHERS OF AMERICA reports one Negro member.

The INTERNATIONAL STEREOTYPERS AND ELECTROTYPERS UNION OF NORTH AMERICA reports 12 Negroes. The experience of the international with Negro members is that "they are loyal, faithful and dependable. They have never acted as strikebreakers even when discriminated against. Negro mechanics in our business are so few that they are negligible in influence. They have acted just like the whites and we have no complaints to make against them either individually or as a race.

However, Union No. 55 of Springfield, Ohio, reports that Negroes are not admitted to membership because in the opinion of that union they are held undesirable because they do not make highly skilled workmen and "because they are not the type for the highly skilled work which our craft class have".

Forty-three Negro workers were found in the INTERNATIONAL PRINTING PRESSMEN AND ASSISTANTS UNION. The international reports that no distinction is made between white and colored, that efforts are made to secure all persons employed in the trade and if they should be colored they are organized on the same standards as the white employees. Despite this statement from the international union, the Denver Printing Pressmen's Union No. 46 does not now admit Negroes to membership. Some time ago a Negro member of this union resigned after "being repeatedly asked to do so".

The INTERNATIONAL TYPOGRAPHICAL UNION "has never recognized a color line and the applicant for membership in the organization must have served five years in the trade and be a competent printer".[1] Replies from 33 locals of this organization, covering 30 per cent of its total membership, show 128 Negro members located in Milwaukee, Wisconsin, Spokane,

[1] Wolfe in "Admission to American Trade Unions," (p. 118), points out that the earliest recorded case of trade union opposition to Negro workers was that of the New Orleans Typographical Society. In 1834 this organization forbade its members to work with a free man of color either as a compositor or as a pressman.

Washington, District of Columbia, New York City, Toledo, Ohio and St. Paul, Minnesota. In Perth Amboy, N. J., there is one Negro apprentice.

At the 1912 convention of the International a Negro was the delegate from a local union in Bay City, Michigan.

The secretary of Local Union No. 523, Tarrytown (N. Y.) comments on the absence of Negro members in the typographical union as follows:

"As my memory serves me we have had but one Negro in our list of members in the last twenty years. As to any distinction being made between whites and Negroes, I am unable to say just what would occur should an occasion of that kind arise. I have no doubt that there would be objections raised as to the admission of a Negro, and this only on account of our experience with the gentleman that we had as a member about twenty years ago.

"The Negro does not seem to take kindly to the printing business, as I have no recollection of the employment of any in the past twenty years excepting the gentleman I spoke of—write of—would sound better.

"In connection with the above paragraph, it is my belief that the reason for the condition mentioned does not lay at the feet of the whites, but is the fault of the Negro himself. The printing business requires a person of more than average intelligence in order to get along and make a success of his work. In this, in most instances, the Negro is lacking. This condition may not be universal, but it is the condition in our jurisdiction. They do not seem to be inclined to stay in school long enough to complete the necessary studies to equip them to cope with the whites, that is as applying to the printing business. Of course there are parts of the printing business that any one of them might fit in very acceptably. But the operation of Typesetting machines, etc., does not seem to appeal to them.

"But I believe that the Negro should be organized. I believe that by so doing he will gain a better livelihood, and that his working conditions will be better also."

The secretary of the Ashtabula, Ohio, local writes "to my knowledge no Negro has attained that degree of education to take up the printing trade. The secretary-treasurer of Union No. 658 in Perth Amboy, N. J., writes: "I worked in . . .

New York in 1906 during the strike there in the *Daily Standard*
The one colored member of the local went out with the
rest of the crew. Although much pressure was used to get
him back, and a number of white men gave up their union cards
and returned to work, the Negro remained true to his obligations and finally had to walk out of town, but he walked out
whistling—a true man".

No colored members were found in various locals of the
INTERNATIONAL BROTHERHOOD OF BOOKBINDERS.

PUBLIC SERVICE

In an analysis of the NATIONAL FEDERATION OF FEDERAL
EMPLOYEES UNION which covered 15,000 members, 2,008 Negroes
were located. These were found in Washington, D. C., Buffalo,
N. Y., Chicago, New York City, Philadelphia, St. Paul, Minnesota,
and other cities.

Federal Union No. 2 of Washington, D. C., admits Negro
members but discourages their joining. However in the capitol
city, Negro workers do not join as rapidly as is desirable because
of low wages and because they are barred from social activities.
In that city there is a separate Negro Local No. 71, the membership
of which is recruited from all departments of the government.
While the white members are organized on the basis of employment in particular governmental departments. Negroes belong
both to the separate local and to the departmental organizations.

The majority of the members of Local No. 71 (the colored
local) were at one time members of Federal Employees Union
No. 2 which is a mixed local. Following the World War it appears
that a situation developed which caused much dissatisfaction
among the colored members of Local No. 2. Quite a number of
colored government employees were dropped from the service—
some of whom were officers of the union. Colored members were
given no recognition at all, they were overlooked at meetings and
apparently no attention was paid to them. No information as to
the cause for such procedure was given to these members. Because
of the strained relationship existing between the two races in this
local, most of the colored members decided to withdraw and build
up a separate organization, which was chartered in 1919 as Local
No. 71. At the September 1927 convention of the Federal Employees, Local No. 2 introduced a resolution advocating separate
locals for the two races in government service.

In New York, Negroes have been members of Union No. 4 since its organization. They are active and responsive in meetings and show a fine spirit. Mixed banquets are held and the union is particularly impressed with the fact that the type of colored employees is exceptionally high, which accounts for the fact that many of the officials in local unions are Negroes. In Philadelphia 300 of the 1,900 members are Negroes. The relationship existing between the two is cordial—both races meeting together and have the same privileges and opportunities.

The INTERNATIONAL ASSOCIATION OF FIRE FIGHTERS reports a membership of 20,000. In a canvass of 9 locals covering 1,217 members 18 Negres were found. As membership is dependent upon employment in the fire department of incorporated municipalities, the non-employment of Negro firemen in many cities is responsible for this exclusion. Negro members were reported in New York, N. Y., Kanas City, Mo., Pittsburgh, Pa. St. Paul, Minn., and Dayton, Ohio.

Though volunteer fire fighters are not eligible to membership in this body the fact that exclusion of Negroes is practiced within such a group is of interest. The Goodwill Fire Company, of Darby, Pa., a Negro organization of volunteer fire fighters was admitted to the Delaware County Firemen's Association after a long discussion by a vote of 51 to 49. Those opposing the admission of Negro fire fighters were members of the Media, Pa., companies that restricted membership to white males over twenty-one years of age.[1]

The AMERICAN FEDERATION OF TEACHERS reports a membership of 3,500 and a Negro membership that is negligible. A canvass of one-fourth of its membership revealed 11 Negro members. According to the general secretary-treasurer of this union, the American Federation of Teachers from its beginning in 1916 has had no desire to draw the color line in its membership. Even at that time there were a few colored members among the elementary teachers in Chicago. The first local charter issued by the American Federation of Teachers after its organization was that of the colored high school teachers of the District of Columbia which became Local No. 9. Later there was a local of colored elementary teachers in the District of Columbia, No. 27. There followed an organization of colored normal teachers and elementary teachers in Washington, D. C.,

---

[1] Associated Negro Press Dispatch, March 6, 1925.

Atlanta, Ga., San Antonio, Texas, and two or three in Oklahoma. The largest and best established of these organizations were the ones of the District of Columbia and San Antonio, Texas, teachers. None of these existed in 1926 with the possible exception of the elementary teachers in the District of Columbia which was not in good standing with the American Federation of Teachers.

Two probable reasons are given for the decline of these locals. The first that officers have been arbitrary, attempting to conduct the affairs of the local without the knowledge or assistance of the membership. In Washington, the high school local went out of existence because of the haughty attitude of the local officers who were in charge of the group of twenty-five or thirty members. The second reason for the failure of these locals is the poor economic condition of colored teachers. More than 100 were functioning as a local in San Antonio with the assistance of the white local, and all would have gone well had not opposition in its most pronounced form arisen.

The method of organizing Negro teachers is based upon local conditions. In southern cities they are usually organized in separate locals. In Minneapolis, the secretary of Local No. 59 states that "in our profession teachers, school boards and superintendents of schools belong to the same group. Race prejudice is as liable to be found in the mind of the official as in that of the teacher. The employer in our case would feel that he was elevating Negroes to his own social level if he employed them as teachers."

In New York while Local Union No. 5 has not been very successful in securing Negro memberships, it was particularly successful in preventing the er ction of a Negro trade school in Harlem which was an acknowledged Jim Crow plan. In Memphis, Tennessee, there is complete separation of the races and no union of colored teachers. In Chicago "a great many" colored teachers belong to the union, but few attend the meetings. Because the New York delegates to the 1929 convention of the American Federation of Teachers which convened in Chicago, introduced resolutions urging equality for white and Negro pupils and teachers, "strife was evinced" within the resolution committee of that body. Local No. 5 of New York also sought to have the Federation endorse a special campaign to unionize Negro teachers and to resolve that Negro and white teachers be organized in the same locals.

The NATIONAL FEDERATION OF POST OFFICE CLERKS admits all Negroes to membership, and in 1926 had only two locals composed entirely of Negroes. These locals were located in Washington, D. C., Local No. 148, and Jacksonville, Florida, Local No. 492. Large memberships of Negro clerks were reported in Chicago and New York. The organization does not employ any organizers, this work being undertaken by the officers and individual parties who volunteer for this service. This applies to all members regardless of race. Local No. 148 in Washington had in 1928, 123 members. The total Negro membership of this union is estimated at 2,000.

The AMALGAMATED PUBLIC SERVICE WORKERS UNION of New York reported in 1926 a total membership of 700 of whom 70 were Negroes.

FOOD, LIQUOR AND TOBACCO

The INTERNATIONAL UNION OF BAKERY AND CONFECTIONERY WORKERS believes that bakers should organize regardless of race, color or creed. The relationship between white and colored at conventions is said to be "splendid". The colored membership is limited because southerners object to meeting with Negroes. As a result, the Bakers Union has set up separate locals composed of Negroes in Charleston, S. C. The international secretary reports that "in my opinion the only reason that the membership of colored bakery workers is so limited is because of the fact that generally unorganized conditions prevail in our industry throughout the southern states where Negro workers predominate." We regret that in some instances there is opposition to jointly meeting with these workers, and that to a considerable extent has been a drawback in bringing them into the organization. In Chicago Negroes were used to break strikes some years ago and that situation remains unsettled. In cases where a special local is desired and feasible, Negro workers are said to enjoy the same privileges and rights as in other locals.

However, in San Francisco, Bakers' Local No. 24 has discouraged Negro workers from joining, despite the fact that at least once a year a Negro worker applies for membership. The Trenton, N. J. Local No. 261 voted at its meeting on February 20, 1926 not to admit Negroes in its local. In Charleston, S. C., there is a local of 65 Negroes. In Winona, Minnesota, Local No. 118 reports 125 members. The financial secretary writes:

"We have two colored bakers as members, getting the same pay as the whites. Then we have the rest as bakers' helpers, about five Negro women who prepare fruit in the pie bakeries getting the same wages as men, and three colored men as ice-cream workers getting the same pay as white. The only trouble I find with the colored members is that though receiving the same benefits as all the white, they are constantly behind with their dues."

In its southern field the Bakers' Union experienced great difficulty. It was never possible to organize permanent mixed locals in the South. The whites refused to remain in locals into which Negroes were admitted. In many cases they expressed their unwillingness to belong to the same international union. Because they were unable to promote this type of organization, the officers decided to issue separate charters to white and Nergo locals respectively. [1]

In Spokane, Washington, Local No. 74 has no Negro members at present, but, according to the secretary, there is "a Mexican member who is married to a Negro woman, who is accorded the same treatment as other members in every way. Several years ago we had two Negro members who were good union men, but they left here to return to southern states because employers would not give them any steady employment. The employers maintained that their customers objected to eating products produced by Negroes. I remember that at an international convention of bakery workers in Cleveland, Ohio, considerable disturbance was caused when a show there refused admittance to Negro delegates. The bakery workers generally favor the organization of Negroes not into separate unions, but as regular members of all unions." One hundred and ninety Negro members were located in ten locals of this union.

The INTERNATIONAL UNION OF BREWERY. FLOUR AND CEREAL AND SOFT DRINK WORKERS OF AMERICA. Despite the fact that Negroes are admited to full membership in this union, the international office reports that the number of Negro members is not known. The organization has been affected by strikes in which both Negroes and whites were involved both as strikers and strikebreakers. Southern white workers have objected to working in the same shops with Negroes and by doing so have limited their organization. The union has made no special ef-

---

[1] Proceedings of the 7th convention of Bakery & Confectionery Workers International Union, September, 1920, p. 8.

fort to secure Negro membership, yet its success in organizing Negroes has been fair, except in the South where Negroes are employed in the soft drink bottling establishments.

Local No. 268 of Newark, New Jersey, reported that a number of Negroes were at one time members of that local, but they declined to continue their membership. No reason was given for this situation.

The AMALGAMATED FOOD WORKERS OF AMERICA reports no Negro members. The objection to the employment of Negro workers in the food industry appears to be centered around the objection of employers who maintain that their products are made less desirable for the public if handled by Negro workers.

The INTERNATIONAL ALLIANCE OF HOTEL AND RESTAURANT EMPLOYEES AND THE BARTENDERS INTERNATIONAL LEAGUE OF AMERICA found it necessary to make provisions for separate local unions because it had been unable to overcome in some sections of the country the unfortunate attitude of white workers toward Negro members. In December 1925, the membership of this organization was given as 38,503 of whom approximately 1,000 were Negroes. "We have had several thousand at one time, but they were scared out by the majority of their employers who probably told them to choose between the union and their job."

"In New York City there is a local union of Negro members which was chartered in 1903, which to the best of my recollection has never had a membership in excess of 50, in fact for the last ten years they have not averaged 20 members. This in spite of the fact that there must be many hundreds of members in New York city. I do not know this to be a fact, but it has been alleged that Local No. 11 of New York City is almost wholly composed of workers employed by Tammany Hall. Persistent endeavor to organize Negroes has been very discouraging. During the war, several Negroes were employed as organizers, but out of approximately 34 unions formed during that period, not one is in existence today. The union regards the organization of the Negro workers as quite essential. In many cases if the Negroes were not organzied, the union would be divided. In Local No. 34 of Boston, Mass., Negroes enjoy the same privileges as their white co-workers, but it required said experience to convert them to united action. The employers played one race against the other, reducing wages and increasing hours, but when the two races formed the union, these conditions were improved."

The circular letter issued by the international union states "where colored workers in the industry desire, they may form local unions of their own race; there is no law which would deny to any local the privilege of accepting colored workers as members."

The local situations vary. The COOKS, PASTRY AND ASSIST-ANTS Union No. 44 of San Francisco does not admit Negro members, whereas the same branch of the union in Mobile, Alabama, is composed entirely of colored. Local No. 59 in Milwaukee, initiates the colored members and transfers them to the nearest local. Local No. 400 in Spokane, Washington, does not admit Negroes. In Chicago, the colored Hotel and Restaurant Employees have their own union. In New York, Waiters Union No. 11 had 16 members in 1926 and was organized only to avoid difficulties with other organizations in the city. The Cooks and Waiters Union does not admit Negroes. That organization, however, appointed its secretary as a special organizer in 1925 to organize Negro workers. This organizer says: "I could not even get them to attend any open meetings to say nothing of becoming organized, so I gave up the idea". The Cleveland Waiters' and Beverage Dispensers' Union does not admit Negro workers, apparently because Negroes at one time served as strikebreakers, defeating the union and retaining their jobs, working for less wages and longer hours. In Denver, Colorado, a separate local of Negro workers did not see the need of organization. Local No. 484 in Chicago, however, has white and colored members. Around 1920 efforts were made to organize Negro restaurants on the South side, but as the Negro workers seemed satisfied with conditions, very little headway was made. The Chicago Waitresses' Union organized in 1902, excludes only Chinese. Negro organizers were used around 1920 at a salary of $300 a month. Waitresses were found working for $2.50 a day, 10 hours a day, and 7 days a week. When a meeting was called, not a waitress attended.

The AMALGAMATED MEAT CUTTERS AND BUTCHER WORK-MEN. Between 1910 and 1920 the number of semi-skilled workmen in slaughtering and packing houses increased more than 1,000 per cent. Though the Meat Cutters and Butcher Workmen has had more than 3,000 Negro members in the mid-western states, that number has now been reduced to 301. In the strike of 1904 Negro and Greek workers were brought in for the unskilled occupations. When unionism was again established in the Chicago stock yards in 1917 there were separate local unions of Negroes, Poles and other nationalities. In a few cases Negro workers were members of mixed unions. The race feeling that existed among the workers, frequently resulting in segregation, made the problem of organization a most difficult one. The failure of an agreement between management and workers has caused the union to again fall to a low membership level as in 1905. One of the national organizers of this union states that "the colored race if given a chance to organize is just as good people as some of the foreigners, and in some cases better."

The INTERNATIONAL UNION OF CIGAR MAKERS. Eighteen unions of this organizatio♦ with a total membership of 4,774 reported 110 Negro members. At one time a Negro was a member of the executive board of this organization. In recent years, however, the Negro membership has declined. In southern states where the larger number of Negro tobacco and cigar workers are located, the trade is not as well organized as in northern states where a larger number of foreign born colored workers are engaged in the trade. The principal cities in the South where Negroes are employed are New Orleans, Louisiana, Tampa, Florida, Key West, Florida. In Memphis, Tennessee, there are three Negro members in Local No. 266. The same number is in Local No. 25, Milwaukee, Wisconsin.

The TOBACCO WORKERS INTERNATIONAL UNION reports a membership of 3,000 of whom 100 are Negroes. It is the opinion of the international office that Negro workers are much more acceptable as members of trade unions when they are organized in separate locals. Otherwise, however, they are admitted on an equal basis. Contradictory to the statement of the International which was made in 1926 is the report from Local Union No. 173 in Winston-Salem, N. C. This is a colored local with a reported membership of 2,975. Workers in this union are said to maintain an agreement with the tobacco firms similar to that maintained by the white organized workers. Up to 1919 there were five colored tobacco workers locals in Winston-Salem. These were united in order to reduce the overhead expense, and to facilitate organization of, and cooperation between colored tobacco workers.

Organization facilities are centered in the factories of the R. J. Reynolds Company in this city, and when 250 colored workers were discharged early in 1928, apparently because of the reduction in labor forces, a representative of the Central Labor Union maintained that these workers were dropped because they and other colored workers in the factory were joining the tobacco workers' union.

An interesting sideline in this connection is the report of an investigator who was in North Carolina during the textile strike, and reported that the chief organizer of the tobacco workers in that district had never been into the colored community, nor did he know exactly where it was located.

AMUSEMENTS

ACTORS' EQUITY ASSOCIATION. This organization limits its membership to persons who have been actors for at least two years. Those persons who have been actors for less than two years and who have played at least one speaking part are eligible to election as junior members. In 1925-26 the Association reported a membership of 10,000. In this number there were 12 Negro members. Negroes are admitted to membership in this organization only when acting in white companies. The secretary of the association writes: "We have always suggested that they form their own branch as we do not understand the conditions of the colored theatres in the South."

The AMERICAN ARTISTES FEDERATION was originally known as the White Rat Actors' Union. A Negro branch of the White Rats existed for nine months during 1916 and 1917, but was split on an issue of discrimination in the clubhouse movement which was attempted at that time.

The AMERICAN FEDERATION OF MUSICIANS estimates that there are approximately 3,000 Negroes members of that union. If the local in a city will not admit Negro members, a separate charter is issued to the Negro group. In many cases it means that Negro musicians work on a lower scale than the white musicians.

Colored locals of this organization existed in the following cities in 1928:

LOCAL No.		LOCAL No.	
44	St. Louis, Mo.	550	Cleveland, Ohio
168	Dallas, Texas	558	Omaha, Neb.
177	Lafayette, Ind.	570	Erie, Pa.
185	Parkersburg, W. Va.	496	New Orleans, La.
208	Chicago, Ill.	584	Paducah, Ky.
242	Youngstown, Ohio	740	Sioux City, Iowa
286	Toledo, Ohio	753	Denver, Colo.
335	Jacksonville, Ill.	813	Zanesville, Ohio
449	Wilmington, Del.	587	Milwaukee, Wis.
465	Mobile, Ala.	589	Columbus, Ohio
471	Pittsburgh, Pa.	591	Philadelphia, Pa.
482	Beaumont, Texas	602	Terre Haute, Ind.
486	New Haven, Conn.	627	Kansas City, Mo.
710	Washington, D. C.	632	Des Moines, Ia.
733	Birmingham, Ala.	635	Dayton, Ohio
782	Springfield, Ohio	648	Oakland, Cal.
493	Seattle, Wash.	666	Martins Ferry, Ohio
513	Houston, Texas	675	Springfield, Ohio
520	Trenton, N. J.	676	Norfolk, Va.
523	Gary, Ind.	681	Salt Lake City, Utah
533	Buffalo, N. Y.	698	Ft. Wayne, Ind.
535	Boston, Mass.	767	Los Angeles, Cal.
534	Baltimore, Md.	775	Richmond, Va.
548	Annapolis, Md.	814	Cincinnati, Ohio

The membership of some of the colored locals at that time was:

Seattle, Washington	43	Omaha No. 558	99
New Haven, Conn.	23	Gary, Ind., No. 523	29
Parkersburg, W. Va.	22	Philadelphia, Pa.	389
Columbus, O., No. 589	112	Baltimore, Md.	140
Martins Ferry, O., No. 666	26	Richmond, Va.	75
Boston No. 535	93	Mobile, Ala.	84

In other localities as in Minneapolis, Minnesota, Lorrain, Ohio, New York, N. Y., Newark, N. J., Rochester, N. Y., Binghampton, N. Y., Jersey City, N. J., New Brunswick, N. J., and San Francisco, California, Negroes are members of white locals.

In Dayton, Ohio, musicians of the Negro local are recognized as are members of any other local of the Federation, and it is permissible to play with them as an organization, "but we do not mix with them in the same band or orchestra or play in the same organization." In Denver, Colorado, Negroes have a separate organization and maintain a wage scale and working conditions lower than that of the white association. In New York where 1,500 of the 13,000 members (January 1, 1926) are Negroes there has never been any trouble professionally or socially. The secretary reports "we frequently have mixed orchestras". In Newark, N. J., where Negroes are members of white locals, "it is very seldom that a Negro musician appears at one of our meetings and when one does attend, he makes no effort to take part in the proceedings."

No Negroes belong to Local No. 163 in Johnstown, N. Y. They have served as strikebreakers in two instances in that city. They have retained control of shops in both of these cases. The Rochester, New York local, despite its mixed membership does not work white and black in the same orchestra. A different situation exists in Superior, Wisconsin. The following United Press Dispatch of January 21, 1930[1] illustrates a jurisdictional dispute into which the problem of color was injected. The travelling Negro orchestra enjoyed an enviable reputation.

"The committee of Fex fraternity at Superior State Teachers College had employed an orchestra whose contract with a promoter did not mention the fraternity.

Local musicians objected and the 300 dancers, in tuxedos and evening dresses, waited while the argument was thrashed out. President Joseph Weber of the American Association of Musicians, wired from New York that the orchestra, a Negro band, could not infringe on rights of local musicians.

"When the dance appeared to be a failure, and the orchestra prepared to leave, an enterprising college youth hired each member separately and the dance went on.

The local musicians said they would take steps to have the Negro members expelled from the union."

At the 34th Annual Convention of the American Federation of Musicians held in Denver, May 1929, the reception accorded colored delegates was described in the *Denver Star* of June 1, 1929 as "another proof that music and art know neither color nor race". Negro delegates walked with respective states in the parade and no segregation was visible.

---

[1] N. Y. Sun, January 21, 1930.

The INTERNATIONAL ALLIANCE OF THEATRICAL STAGE EM-
PLOYEES AND MOVING PICTURE MACHINE OPERATORS OF THE
UNITED STATES AND CANADA grants complete autonomy to all
locals of the organization, which necessarily makes such an organization approach the status of a closed corporation. It is
quite generally the rule or law of the various locals that a
candidate must have two-thirds of the votes of the membership
in order to be elected to that body. While several organizations
report that Negroes are not admitted to membership there appears to be no law which would preclude Negro membership.

The international office reports that approximately 100 of
the 26,000 members of this alliance are Negroes. In some instances, auxiliary charters have been granted to Negro workers
in certain cities. In Chattanooga, Tennessee, the local by-laws
prohibit Negroes from joining the local. In Hagerstown, Md.,
Negro membership is regarded as unnecessary because of the
supply of white labor. In Tacoma, Washington, while there
is no law against Negro membership, apprenticeship for Negroes
would be barred, or the application for a Negro member would
be "ballotted down". This same local favors the organization
of Negroes but would not permit membership in its ranks. In
Baltimore, Maryland, the members of Local No. 181 did not
care to associate with colored workers. It is claimed that Negroes will not join these unions fearing that if theatres are
compelled to pay the same wage to colored operators as to white,
that white operators will be used. A few years ago Local No.
181 had seven or eight theatres organized which catered to colored patrons exclusively. Every year when a new contract was
presented at least two of these theatres were lost because Negroes
accepted employment in them at lower wages than the union
demanded. In 1926 there was only one white member in a
colored house.

New York City has had probably the most interesting experience in the organization of Negro motion picture machine
operators. For at least five years a group of colored operators
known as the United Association of Colored Motion Picture
Operators, who were employed in Harlem and vicinity, had
attempted to secure membership in Local No. 306 of the I. A.
T. S. E. and M. P. M. O. For more than three years their
overtures to the union were of no avail Partly because twelve
colored operators were employed in at least eight theatres in
New York, thereby preventing the organization of that many
theatres by the union, Local No. 306 called a meeting of these

colored operators. As a result of this meeting the following agreement for the establishment of an auxiliary local was submitted to the colored operators.

"As per our meeting of this date, and as per your request, herewith follow the rules as made by the committee of Local No. 306 and which were read to you and your committee at our joint meeting:

1—The Negro operators admitted to this auxiliary must pay the prevailing initiation fee upon admittance. They must pay the same dues as the white members of this local, as well as any assessments levied by our assembly.

2—The Negro operators shall be entitled to all of the privileges enjoyed under our prevailing Wage Scale and Conditions, excepting as follows: The Negro shall be confined as far as is physically possible to working in the colored belt under the jurisdiction of Local No. 306.

3—The Negro operators shall be subject to the provisions of our constitution and by-laws with the following exceptions: The Negro operators will not be permitted to attend the regular meetings of Local No. 306. The President shall appoint a member of Local No. 306 to represent the Negro operators at our regular meetings, said appointment to be approved by the auxiliary members to Local No. 306 for Negro operators. The members so appointed shall also act as the representative of the local at all caucuses of the Auxiliary and the local which he may call at the discretion of the Executive Board of the local. He shall also act as the representative of the auxiliary members to Local No. 306 for Negro operators in all their grievances.

4—The above rules as set forth are made for an indefinite period. After these rules are in effect for a reasonable length of time upon petition properly made to the local and upon the will of our body, the auxiliary members to Local No. 306 may become full-fledged members to Local No. 306 with the following exceptions: They shall not attend the regular meetings of the Union.

5—The above rules as laid down are subject to change at any time at the discretion of the Executive Board of Local No. 306, I. A. T. S. E.

Fraternally submitted,

Recording Secretary."

This overture was promptly rejected by the colored operators. There followed a period of bargaining in which the colored operators were victorious and which finally led to their being accepted as regular members of Local No. 306, without being circumscribed by any of the provisions stated in the above mentioned letter.

MISCELLANEOUS UNIONS

The LAUNDRY WORKERS INTERNATIONAL UNION reported a total membership of 7,000 of whom 11 were Negroes. The union estimates that there are between 20,000 and 30,000 Negroes working in laundries in the southern states none of whom are organized. In the larger local unions in San Francisco and Seattle, Washington, where Negroes form only 1 per cent of the membership they are well liked and no discrimination is shown against them. In some instances where unions have been established in Fort Smith, Arkansas, the organization is weak because of the lack of interest by Negro workers. Attempts to organize Negro laundry workers in New York have been only partially successful. Local No. 110 in Washington, D. C. has a total membership of 100 all of whom are Negroes. This union was organized in 1916 and is composed of all of the colored laundry workers in the Bureau of Engraving and Printing.

The JOURNEY BARBERS INTERNATIONAL UNION reports a membership of 54,000. A canvass of 9 per cent of its membership revealed 239 Negro members. The policy of the international union is to admit Negroes to full membership without any distinction whatsoever. Its organization policy enables Negroes to be organized in separate or in mixed local unions. One Negro organizer is employed by the International.

One of the problems facing the organization of Negro barbers, however, is that fact that unless they are catering to white trade or working in white shops, it is impossible for them to maintain a wage scale similar to that demanded by the local union. For this reason Negro membership is a fluctuating one. The colored local in Chattanooga, Tennessee, which had 50 members in 1927 had 12 in 1928. The reason for this decrease is said to be the objection on the part of Negro barbers to the restrictions placed upon them by the union. The Negro barbers wished to work as long as they pleased and on Sunday as well. They feared that union prices would operate against their trade in colored shops. The first barbers' local in this city was a mixed one and when in the first election of officers some colored members won places, the whites who opposed colored officers made conditions so disagreeable for colored members that a separation was agreed upon and colored and whites decided to have separate unions. White barbers will not associate with colored barbers in the same local in that section. Colored members in mixed unions were found in Akron, Ohio, Minneapolis, Minnesota, Chicago, Illinois, Huntington, W. Va., Dayton, Ohio, Cleveland, Ohio, Cincinnati, Ohio, Troy, N. Y., Bridgetown, N. Y., and St. Paul, Minnesota.

The INTERNATIONAL BROOM AND WHISK MAKERS UNIONS estimates that there are about 50 Negro members of that organization in Chicago. There has been a mixed local of this organization for many years and according to the general secretary-treasurer there has never been any quarrel or trouble between the Negro and white members.

Local No. 76 of the Upholsterers Union, New York, reports 4 Negro members, while Local No. 70 of the Upholsterers and Linoleum Layers is said to refuse to admit Negro workers.[1] Local No. 2035 of the Furniture Workers reports 4 Negro members in a total of 200.

The INTERNATIONAL JEWELRY WORKERS UNION reports 50 Negro members, the majority of whom are found in the novelty branch of the industry. In meetings colored workers do not take a very active part, show very little expression of interest and do not appear comfortable. Jewish workers are said to be in the majority in this industry, closely followed by Italians. Negroes and natives white workers form the remaining portion

The PAPER BOX MAKERS UNION OF GREATER NEW YORK was involved in a city wide strike in 1927. It reports a total membership of 2500 of whom 50 are Negroes.

The AMALGAMATED SILVER WORKERS UNION, the INTERNATIONAL FEDERATION OF TECHNICAL ENGINEERS, ARCHITECTS AND DRAFTSMEN, the BILL POSTERS AND BILLERS and the INTERNATIONAL WOOD CARVERS ASSOCIATION report no Negro members.

Two locals of the BOOK-KEEPERS, STENOGRAPHERS AND ACCOUNTANTS UNION No. 16456 report no Negro members. New York Local No. 12646 has had as many as 5 Negro members.

---

[1] Red Bank (N. J.) Echo. December 15, 1929.

Efforts have been made by this organization to organize Negro clerical workers but without much success.

In the New York SIGN WRITERS UNION No. 239 there are 10 Negro members. The secretary reports that all Negroes in this craft are members of the union, and that there is no complaint or dissatisfaction regarding their affiliation.

The RETAIL CLERKS' INTERNATIONAL PROTECTIVE ASSOCIATION reports that Negroes are admitted to membership except in San Diego, California, where Local No. 769 states that its constitution prohibits the membership of Negro clerks.

Local No. 17797 of the CLEANERS, DYERS AND PRESSMEN'S UNION in New York, composed of men who do the "inside" work in cleaning establishments has 200 Negro members, while the Chicago local of the same union reports 1500 Negroes. There are no Negro workers in the CLEANING AND DYE HOUSE PRESSERS UNION No. 813. In the DYERS AND MERCERIZERS UNION No. 1, Philadelphia, there are no Negro members. Local No. 17831 of the POST OFFICE LABORERS UNION in San Francisco reports 15 Negro members out of a total membership of 100. The WINDOW CLEANERS PROTECTIVE UNION Local No. 8 of the BUILDING SERVICE EMPLOYEES INTERNATIONAL ASSOCIATION have "quite a number of colored workers, but the great majority of them are still unorganized."

TABLE X

Negro Membership in American Trade Unions*
1890, 1900, 1926, 1928

UNION	NEGRO MEMBERSHIP			
	1890[10]	1900[10]	1910[11]	1926-28
Actors and Artists	—	—	—	12
Automobile, Aircraft and Vehicle Workers[1]	240	500	1,000	50
Bakery and Confectionery Workers	—	—	—	190
Barbers	200	800	1,000	239
Blacksmiths, Drop Forgers and Helpers	—	—	—	—
Boot and Shoe Workers	—	—	50	50
Brewery, Flour and Cereal Workers	—	—	10	—
Bricklayers, Masons and Plasterers	—	—	—	1,917
Brick and Clay Workers[2]	50	200	—	100
Bridge and Structural Iron Workers	—	—	—	2
Broom and Whisk Makers	—	—	6	50
Building Service Employees	—	—	—	70
Carmen, Railway	—	—	—	500
Carpenters and Joiners	—	1,000	2,500	1,572
Carvers, Wood	—	—	—	—
Cigar Makers	—	—	5,000	110
Cleaners, Dyers and Pressers[3]	—	—	—	1,500
Clerks, Post Office[7]	—	—	—	356
Cloth, Hat, Cap and Millinery Workers	—	—	—	300
Clothing Workers, Amalgamated	—	—	—	Very few
Compressed Air Foundation Workers	—	200	—	700
Coopers	—	200	—	—
Electric Workers	—	—	—	1
Elevator Constructors	—	—	(A few)	10
Engineers, Operating[4]	—	—	—	1,200
Engravers, Photo	—	—	6	2
Federal Employees	—	—	—	2,008
Firemen and Oilers[5]	—	2,700	—	150
Fire Fighters	—	—	—	18
Foundry Employees	—	—	—	150
Fur Workers	—	—	—	11
Furniture Workers	—	—	—	4
Garment Workers, International Ladies	—	—	—	519
Garment Workers	—	—	—	130
Glove Workers	—	—	—	2
Granite Cutters	—	—	—	2

TABLE X (Continued)

UNION	NEGRO MEMBERSHIP			
	1890[10]	1900[10]	1910[11]	1926-28
Hod Carriers, Building and Common Laborers	—	—	—	10,131
Hotel and Restaurant Employees	—	—	2,500	1,000
Iron, Steel and Tin Workers	—	—	3	300
Jewelry Workers	—	—	—	50
Lathers, Wood, Wire and Metal	—	—	—	223
Laundry Workers	—	—	—	111
Leather Workers, U. I. U.	—	—	—	8
Letter Carriers	—	—	—	1,376
Lithographers	—	—	—	1
Longshoremen	1,500	6,000	—	12,381
Mail Association, Railway	—	—	—	6
Maintenance of Way Employees	—	—	—	10,000
Meat Cutters and Butcher Workmen	—	—	—	301
Metal Workers, Amalgamated[6]	—	—	—	12
Metal Workers, Sheet	—	—	—	7
Mine Workers, United	—	20,000	40,000[9]	5,000
Mine, Mill and Smelter Workers	—	—	—	500
Molders	—	—	12	12
Musicians	—	—	—	3,000
Painters, Decorators and Paper Hangers	33	169	—	718
Paper Makers	—	—	—	—
Paving Cutters	—	—	—	310
Piano and Organ Workers	—	—	1	—
Plasterers (Operative)	—	—	—	782
Printing Pressmen and Assistants	—	—	6	43
Pulp, Sulphite and Paper Mill Workers	—	—	—	1
Railway Employees, Street and Electric	—	—	—	16
Roofers, Damp and Waterproof	—	—	—	19
Seamen	—	—	—	8
Sign Writers	—	—	—	10
Signalmen, Railway	—	—	—	2
Stage Employees and Moving Picture Machine Operators	—	—	4	100
Steam Shovel and Dredgemen	—	—	—	15
Stereotypers and Electrotypers	—	—	—	12
Stone Cutters	—	—	—	2
Tailors, Journeymen	—	—	—	17
Teachers	—	—	—	31
Teamsters and Chauffeurs	—	—	6,000	313
Textile Workers	—	—	—	4
Tobacco Workers	1,500	1,000	—	100

TABLE X (Continued)

Union	Negro Membership			
	1890[10]	1900[10]	1910[11]	1926-28
Tunnel and Subway Workers[8]	——	——	——	600
Typographical Union	——	——	250	128
Upholsterers	——	——	——	4
Negro Locals directly affiliated to the A. F. of L. (excluding Sleeping Car Porters 1926-28)	——	——	309	453
Federal Labor Union No. 17261 Virgin Islands	——	——	——	1000
TOTAL	3,523	32,769	57,662	61,032
Organized Negro Workers in localities not included in above totals	——	——	——	5,041
Sleeping Car Porters	——	——	——	3,000
Independent Negro Unions	——	——	——	12,585
GRAND TOTAL				81,658

* The membership figures for 1890, 1900 and 1910 are estimates from the sources quoted and are not wholly comparable with the 1926-1928 figures.

1 Until 1918 this union was known as the International Union of Wagon and Carriage Workers. It is not affiliated to the A. F. of L.

2 Known as International Alliance of Brick, Tile and Terra Cotta Workers until 1915.

3 Local Unions affiliated to the A. F. of L.

4 The Operating Engineers and the Steam Shovel and Dredgemen amalgamated in 1927.

5 Known as International Brotherhood of Stationary Firemen until 1902.

6 Died out in 1927.

7 The total membership is that of the two unions having jurisdiction in this field.

8 Merged with the International Hod Carriers Union in 1929.

9 Figure given by Wolfe. This number in all probability incorrect as only 39,530 Negroes were employed as coal mine operatives in 1910. Harris (op. cit.) opines that this membership was probably 4,000.

10 Adapted from "The American Negro Artisan," Atlanta University Publications No. 7.

11 Adapted from "The Negro in the American Labor Movement," Harris and Spero.

LOCAL TRADE AND FEDERAL TRADE UNIONS

When in 1900 President Gompers suggested that the Federation organize Negro workers into separate unions and central bodies the racial separation of workers in Labor organizations became more pronounced. In 1902 the convention provided that the Federation might issue separate charters to Central Labor Unions, Local Unions and Federal Labor Unions composed of Negro workers. Thus, Article XI, Section 6 of the Constitution of the American Federation of Labor reads:

"Separate charters may be issued to Central Labor Unions, Local Unions, or Federal Labor Unions composed exclusively of colored members, where, in the judgment of the Executive Council, it appears advisable and to the best interests of the Trade Union Movement to do so."

Each member of a local trade or federal labor union is required to take the following obligation:

"I am to be respectful in work and action to every woman, to be considerate to the widows and orphans, the weak and defenseless, and never to discriminate against a fellow worker on account of creed, color or nationality."

Because of the failure of the Brotherhood of Railway and Steamship Clerks to admit Negro workers, the Federation assumed the responsibility for organizing the Negro freight handlers and station employees who came under the union's jurisdiction. The net result was that the number of Negro local unions directly affiliated to the Federation showed a tremendous growth. In December, 1911, 2 Negro central bodies and 11 local and federal unions with 309 members were affiliated to the Federation. Three salaried Negroes were being employed to organize Negro workers. President Gompers stated in 1919 "Of the 900 Unions affiliated directly to the American Federation of Labor there are 169 composed exclusively of Negroes."

Such labor unions included groups ordinarily affected by the restrictions of national unions. Examples of the types of locals are freight handlers, boilermakers, blacksmith and machinists helpers, coach and car cleaners, railway mail handlers, baggage handlers, platform railway express handlers, truckers, machinists, boilermakers and helpers, and baggagemen. Miscellaneous unions included crab pickers, domestic workers, hair dressers, laborers, janitors, oystermen, train porters, railway clerks and railroad mechanics helpers.

The effectiveness of such organizations has not been the most commendable. Though there were 109 Negro locals affiliated directly to the A. F. of L. in 1919 there were only 52 in 1925 and 38 in 1929. An analysis of the 38 organizations now listed shows that 14 are groups of the recently affiliated Sleeping Car Porters, while 7 of the remaining locals may be classified as inactive. [1]

[1] The 1929 Handbook of American Trade Unions reports 21 directly affiliated local unions covering colored workers.

TABLE XI

Negro Membership in Local Trade and Federal Labor Unions—1928-1929

NUMBER OF UNION	TRADE COMPOSITION	LOCATION	MEMBERSHIP
17053	Freight Handlers	Washington, D. C.	—
17603	Boilermakers, Pipe Fitters and Machinists' Helpers	Jacksonville, Fla.	30
17980	Freight Handlers	Tampa, Fla.	24
17987	Freight Handlers and Station Employees	Jacksonville, Fla.	—
17803	Station Porters	Savannah, Ga.	15
17769[1]	Freight Handlers and Station Employees	Kansas City, Kan.	—
16665	Freight Handlers and Station Employees	Brunswick, Md.	12
16381[2]	Freight Handlers and Station Employees	Baltimore, Md.	—
17393	Freight Handlers and Station Employees	Baltimore, Md.	60
17775[3]	Freight Handlers and Station Employees	Kansas City, Mo.	10
17919	Federal Labor Union		
17523	Freight Handlers and Express and Station Employees	Newark, N. J.	10
17165	Freight Handlers	Wilmington, N. C.	29
17210	Freight Handlers	Cleveland, Ohio	48
17985	Freight Handlers	Sumter, S. C.	17
16324	Freight Handlers	Columbia, S. C.	41
16953	Freight Handlers	Charleston, S. C.	100
17987	Freight Handlers	Providence, R. I.	—
17786	Freight Handlers	San Antonio, Texas	—
18040	Freight Handlers	Pensacola, Fla.	13
17634	Express Handlers	Houston, Texas	30
17658	Freight Handlers and Station Employees	Richmond, Va.	—
17766	Navy Yard Helpers	Portsmouth, Va.	—
18068	Sleeping Car Porters	Norfolk, Va.	14
18070	Sleeping Car Porters	New York, N. Y.	
18077	Sleeping Car Porters	Chicago, Ill.	

[1] The Central Labor Office of Kansas City, Kansas, has no record of Local No. 17769 reported by the Federation as being organized of Freight Handlers and Station Employees.

[2] Attempts to secure the membership of Federal Union No. 16381 were futile.

[3] Local No. 17775 of Kansas City, Missouri, is not a Negro local but a mixed union with 15 white and 10 colored members.

TABLE XI (Continued).

NUMBER OF UNION	TRADE COMPOSITION	LOCATION	MEMBERSHIP
	Brought forward		3,000
18078	Sleeping Car Porters	Kansas City, Mo.	
18088	Sleeping Car Porters	St. Paul, Minn.	
18079	Sleeping Car Porters	Denver, Colo.	
18085	Sleeping Car Porters	Oakland, Cal.	
	Sleeping Car Porters	Los Angeles, Cal.	
18080	Sleeping Car Porters	Omaha, Neb.	
18097	Sleeping Car Porters	Washington D. C.	
	Sleeping Car Porters	Boston, Mass.	
18089	Sleeping Car Porters	New Orleans, La.	
18075	Sleeping Car Porters	Fort Worth, Texas	
18076	Sleeping Car Porters	St. Louis, Mo.	
17991	Post Office Laborers..	Detroit, Mich.	
	TOTAL MEMBERSHIP		3,000
		St. Louis, Mo.	—
17261	Federal Labor Union		3,453[1]
		St. Thomas, V. I.	1,000
	GRAND TOTAL		4,453

Because of the absence of effective machinery in governing these locals and, because of the unsound economic policy in organizing a group of workers whose bargaining power is in many cases weaker than that of a white organization of the same craft, the present status of the Negro local union in collective bargaining is questionable. For example, the financial secretary of the Freight Handlers No. 17786 where 13 of the 24 colored men are organized, writes:

"We do not get the same rights as the white help do in no way. Of course we get 14 days off in the summer months without pay and the whites get it off with pay, (14 days) But we pay just as much dues as they do and do more work for the company. We are only getting $3.12 a day for 8 hours, no time and half for overtime. From May to September of each year we only work 5½ days per week."

These local unions realized the grave problem confronting their activity and were consistently bringing them to the atten-

---

[1] Local No. 10167, Baggage Messengers Union of San Francisco, though listed as a Negro local, does *not* admit Negroes "on account of our business transactions with the public." This union makes no effort to secure Negro members and "in our case" does not regard their organization as essential to the success of the labor movement.

tion of the Federation at its conventions. Resolutions expressed complaints existing in the local fields and requested remedial action. In 1920 the Railroad Shop Workers Union No. 16797 of Houston, Texas, composed of colored mechanics and helpers in the six crafts—"machinists, boilermakers, blacksmiths, sheet metal workers, carmen, painters and all trades of wage earners," requested the A. F. of L. to give them the cooperation and support that would enable them to handle their grievances through the international unions. Their specific request was that the colored unions should be included in the international agreements. Members of this union had realized that they were not receiving the full benefits of organization. The convention ruled, however, that these workers were already provided for in the agreements of railroad craft organizations.

In cities where Negro local unions are not admitted to membership in central labor bodies, the Federation has permitted the organization of Negro city centrals. In 1921 there were ten of these city central bodies composed exclusively of Negroes. On January 1, 1929, there were four such bodies. The distribution of these city central bodies for the period 1921-1928 is shown in the following list.

List of Organizations Affiliated to the American Federation of Labor.
Negro City Centrals.

NAME	LOCATION
NOVEMBER 4, 1921	
Central Labor Union	Richmond, Va.
Central Labor Union	Houston, Tex.
Central Labor Union	Ft. Worth, Tex.
Central Labor Union	Jacksonville, Fla.
Central Labor Union	Brunswick, Ga.
	New Orleans, La.
	Charleston, S. C.
Labor Trades Union	Dennison, Tex.
Central Labor Union	Norfolk, Va.
Central Labor Union	Suffolk, Va.
MARCH 15. 1922	
Central Labor Union	Jacksonville, Fla.
	New Orleans, La.
	Pascagoula, Miss.
	Charleston, S. C.
	Ft. Worth, Tex.

List of Organizations Affiliated to the
American Federation of Labor.
Negro City Centrals.
(Continued)

NAME	LOCATION
MARCH 15, 1922	Houston, Tex.
	Norfolk, Va.
	Richmond, Va.
	Suffolk, Va.
Labor Trades Union	Dennison, Tex.
NOVEMBER 12, 1923	
Central Labor Union	Jacksonville, Fla.
Central Labor Union	Charlotte, N. C.
Labor Trades Union	Denison, Tex.
Central Labor Union	Ft. Worth, Tex.
Central Labor Union	Houston, Tex.
Central Labor Union	Norfolk, Va.
Central Labor Union	Richmond, Va.
Central Labor Union	Suffolk, Va.
JANUARY 1, 1925	
Central Labor Union	Jacksonville, Fla.
Central Labor Union	New Orleans, La.
Central Labor Union	Pascagoula, Miss.
Central Labor Union	Ocean Springs, Miss.
JANUARY 1, 1925	
Central Labor Union	Houston, Tex.
Central Labor Union	Ft. Worth, Tex.
Central Labor Union	Suffolk, Va.
Central Labor Union	Richmond, Va..
NOVEMBER 12, 1926	
Central Labor Union	Ft. Worth, Tex.
	Houston, Tex.
	Richmond, Va.
	Suffolk, Va.
DECEMBER 15, 1927	
Central Labor Union	Ft. Worth, Tex.
	Houston, Tex.
	Richmond, Va.
MARCH 15, 1928	Ocean Springs, Miss.
	Ft. Worth, Tex.
	Houston, Tex.

Between November 4, 1921 and January 1, 1929, Negro local unions directly affiliated to the American Federation of Labor decreased from 141 to 23, representing a loss of 513 per cent. In 1921 apart from the organizations of freighthandlers, baggagemen, express and station employees, the Federation had organized other groups of workers as the boilermakers, blacksmiths' and machinists' helpers in Mobile, Alabama; the domestic workers in New Orleans, La.; and Galveston, Texas; janitors and station employees in Ann Harbor, Michigan; hair dressers in Winston-Salem, N. C.; train porters in Charlotte, N. C.; mail handlers in Columbus, Ohio; machinists and boilermakers helpers in El Paso, Texas, and San Antonio, Texas.

In that year 23 Negro unions were located in Texas, 20 in North Carolina, 11 in South Carolina, 9 in Louisiana, and 6 in Georgia. By 1928, however, more than 75 per cent of such trade and federal unions organized for and by Negroes were composed of freighthandlers, express and station employees. It is apparent that the decreased activity of the Federation in organizing Negroes, as well as the waning interest on the part of these workers in organized labor, was responsible for this severe decline. The membership of Negro local unions for the period 1919 through 1929 was as follows:

TABLE XII

Local Trade and Federal Labor Unions Composed Exclusively of Negro Workers and Per Cent of Negro Unions in Total—1919-1929

DATE	TOTAL UNIONS	NEGRO LOCALS	PER CENT NEGRO
1919[1]	900	169	18.7
1921 (Nov. 4)	679	141	20.8
1922 (Mar. 15)	663	131	19.9
1922 (June 1)	592	108	18.2
1923 (Nov. 12)	527	79	14.9
1925 (Jan. 1)	408	41	15.4
1926 Mar. 10)	372	38	11.1
1927 (Dec. 15)	342	23	6.7
1928 (Dec. 31)	377	23	6.1
1929 (Nov.)[2]	383	21	5.4

[1] Gompers, Samuel, quoted in "Negro in Chicago," p. 405.
[2] Handbook of American Trade Unions, p. 6.

In a Federationist editorial on "Federal Unions" the A. F. of L. voices the following opinion on the status of that branch of the organiation which had 373 federal trades and labor unions at the time of the New Orleans convention as compared with 884 such unions in 1919—

"It is obvious, therefore, that during the coming year we need to put emphasis on organizing federal unions in industries now unorganized. From such unions new nationals and internationals will emerge, strengthening the union movement all along the line." [1]

The BROTHERHOOD OF SLEEPING CAR PORTERS. At least four attempts had been made to organize Pullman porters prior to the organization of the Brotherhood of Sleeping Car Porters on August 25, 1925. When, however, the Executive Council of the A. F. of L. in February 1929, decided to issue federal union charters to Pullman porters organized by the Brotherhood of Sleeping Car Porters, the most forward step in organization had been made. Much of the preceding efforts, while creating a deeper consciousness among the porters, had failed largely because the leaders of the movement attempted to remain in the Pullman service while organizing the men.

Ever since the first attempt of porters to organize, the Pullman Company had fostered a company union. The first organization was known as the Pullman Porters Benefit Association. "For twenty-six dollars it gives a porter death and sick benefits. Should a porter leave the service, his dues are increased 50 per cent, although his risk is considerably less since he is no longer on the road. The increase in dues is calculated to discourage the porter from supposedly risking his job by joining a union." The demands of the Brotherhood as stated in a pamphlet issued in 1927 are—

1—A minimum wage of $150 a month instead of the $72.50 now in effect.

2—A 240-hour month as maintained by the Pullman conductors instead of the approximately 400 hour month now being completed.

3—Pay for preparatory and terminal times (porters receive no pay for time spent in preparing cars and receiving and discharging passengers).

---

[1] The American Federationist, December, 1928—Vol. 35, No. 12, December, 1928.

4—Adjustment of time for delayed arrivals of train.

5—Adjustment of the doubling out system whereby a porter who has returned from his regular run may be "doubled out" on another run without a rest period and at a lower rate of pay than if he were on the regular run.

6—Four hours sleep on the first night out, 6 hours on the second and third nights. (In support of this demand the Brotherhood claims that "on the New York to Key West, Florida and return run, the conductor and the porter leave New York for four days and four nights of work—the length of this run. On the first night the porter is allowed a maximum of three hours sleep and the conductor a minimum of five hours; on the second night the porter is allowed no sleep at all, while the conductor is relieved and sleeps all night; on the the third night the same conditions prevail; on the fourth night, the porter is again allowed three hours and the conductor five hours. Therefore, on the run of 96 hours, less the few hours spent in Key West, the porter is allowed a total of six hours sleep, whereas the conductor is allowed two full nights and ten hours. When the two workers return to New York, the porter is allowed four rest days and the conductor five."

7—The Brotherhood demands conductors pay when the work of a conductor is added to that of porter. It is estimated that there are several thousand porters in charge who, in addition to their own work, must do all the work required of the conductor. For this extra work the porter receives an extra pay of ten dollars a month.

8—A flat rate of pay for extra porters.

9—An adjustment in the purchasing of equipment by the porters. Porters are required to buy the shoe polish equipment for shining passengers shoes, they are required to buy their own uniforms until they have been in the service ten years, they must buy all their own meals on the road. (Though served at half price in the diner the custom requires that they must tip the waiter at every meal.)

10—That the tipping of Pullman porters by the general public be abolished. The Brotherhood finally asks that it, rather than the company union, be recognized as the spokesmen of porters and maids in negotiating agreements, handling grievances and transacting other business between the management and workers.

For four years the Brotherhood of Sleeping Car Porters has waged a continuous fight for recognition of the 12,000 porters and maids by the Pullman Company. Attempts to have the Inter-State Commerce Commission rule on the matter of tipping as a violation of the Inter-state commerce act were futile. The ruling of the Commission was to the effect that the complaint "in all of its aspects leads only to the conclusion that the real objectives sought are increased wages for the porters and maids in the defendant's employ".[1] The Commission ruled that because it had no power to regulate wages, and, secondly, no authority to inquire in the justness of wages, however meritorious such demands might be, the motion of the defendant's to dismiss would be sustained and the complaint dismissed for want of jurisdiction.

The organization of the Brotherhood of Sleeping Car Porters has extended from the Atlantic to the Pacific Coast. During the earlier days of its organization several conferences were held and the support of many outstanding persons and institutions secured on the basis of the right and necessity for organization of this working group. Through the medium of the *Messenger Magazine*, the Pullman porters voiced their objections and the difficulties and problems of this new movement. Meanwhile, jurisdictional disputes were arising. The A. F. of L. was lethargic in rendering such support as would have been of value. The American Negro Labor Congress rose in objection to certain of the steps taken by the Brotherhood in attempting organization. Rumor spread the belief that the Pullman Company would recognize the Brotherhood, providing that its general organizer, A. Phillip Randolph —who had been an active Socialist—be removed from office. Certain Negro newspapers that formerly supported the organization switched their support—other papers opposed to the movement began falling in line. Finally, intercessions with the A. F. of L. provoked the recognition of that organization as a member of the A. F. of L. through the chartering of its several locals as federal unions. Despite the fact that the Brotherhood of Sleeping Car Porters wished recognition as a national union, the jurisdictional claims of the Hotel and Restaurant Employees Association prevented such action.

The opinion of the Federation was that the porters were not strong enough to function nationally. Therefore "instead of issuing to the brotherhood a charter of affiliation to the American

---

[1] The report of the Interstate Commerce Commission No. 2007. Brotherhood of Sleeping Car Porters vs. Pullman Company. Submitted January 21, 1928—decided March 5, 1928.

Federation of Labor, the Federation has chartered under its own immediate jurisdiction, as directly affiliated local unions, the locals of porters which had formerly composed the brotherhood".[1] It is estimated that the present membership is 3,000.

The 1929 convention of the A. F. of L. brought to light additional difficulties faced by the Brotherhood of Sleeping Car Porters and the Hotel and Restaurant Employees Association on the question of jurisdiction. The protests of this national union are recorded in the minutes of the Federation's sessions as follows:[2]

Resolution No. 32 submitted by delegates Edward Flore, Robert E. Kesketch, Conrad Scholte, Emmanuel Koveleski, and Agnes M. Quinn of the Hotel and Restaurant Employees International Alliance and Bartenders International League of America:

Whereas, The subject matter hereto attached covering the jurisdiction over sleeping car porters was submitted to the Twenty-fifth General Convention of the Hotel and Restaurant Employees and Beverage Dispensers International Alliance in August, 1929, and by them unanimously adopted;

Therefore, Be it resolved that the Executive Council of the A. F. of L. be instructed and is hereby directed to turn over to the Hotel and Restaurant Employees and Beverage Dispensers International Alliance such organizations of sleeping car porters now chartered by them as local and federal unions; and

Be it Further Resolved, That in cooperation with the Hotel and Restaurant Employees and Beverage Dispensers International Alliance they continue their efforts to organize and improve the standards of the sleeping car employees.

In support of this resolution the Alliance submitted subject matter showing that the organization had made previous attempts to organize Negro workers in the Pullman service. It appears that on March 2, 1928, the A. F. of L. asked the Hotel and Restaurant Employees Alliance if Negro workers were admitted to membership and if any restrictions were imposed upon them; to which the Alliance replied that no distinctions were made between white and colored workers, furthermore the Hotel and Restaurant Employees Alliance offered to recommend the keeping

---

[1] Handbook, cit. p. 6.
[2] American Federation of Labor Report of Proceedings, 1929—pages 385-86.

of their branch of the trade in a separate unit under the control and operation of men of their choosing, but this offer was refused by the Brotherhood of Sleeping Car Porters because it appeared that "the men in control of that organization desired to keep the colored man aside to himself." Subsequent correspondence covering the issue follows:

"I am enclosing you a part of the records of our last convention held in Portland, Oregon, in August, 1927. It should prove interesting as applied to this subject.

"The workers employed in the sleeping car service are welcome to become a part of the Hotel and Restaurant Employees International Alliance and Bartenders International League of America, either by individual or group affiliation, with the same rights and privileges that are accorded other members.

"We respectfully ask that the American Federation of Labor refer the application for membership of sleeping car employees to our organization, they are a part of the hotel industry and as such come under the jurisdiction of the Hotel and Restaurant Employees organization."

On April 4th, 1928, President Green advised that Brotherhood of Sleeping Car Porters had filed an application for affiliation and that it would be referred to the Executive Council for consideration. We made answer to this letter as follows:

April 12, 1928.

"I have your favor of the 4th in which you advise that the Brotherhood of Sleeping Car Porters had filed an application for a charter of affiliation with the American Federation of Labor which you intend to refer to the Executive Council at their meeting of April 24th. The application sets forth the reason for making said application and you ask that we submit in response, arguments sustaining our claim to that jurisdiction.

"We addressed a letter to you under date of April 3, 1928, covering this subject and enclosed a part of our convention records of 1927, which indicated our activity in connection with the sleeping car employees.

"We do not feel that this office has a right to assume the full responsibility in connection with answering in detail the arguments presented in the application as submitted by Mr. A. Phillip Randolph and his associates. Our general executive board will meet on May 21, 1928, and if the Executive Council will lay this application of the Brotherhood of Sleeping Car Porters over until they have an opportunity to prepare a statement in response and to take such other action as may be necessary in the premises, we will appreciate the courtesy."

The subject matter was referred to the General Executive Board, at its meeting in May, 1928, and the following response was ordered sent to the American Federation of Labor:

"The General Executive Board of our International Union, during its session the week of May 14-19, considered the subject brought to its attention by President Flore with regard to the application of the Brotherhood of Sleeping Car Porters for a charter as an organization directly affiliated to the American Federation of Labor.

"The General Executive Board of our organization contends that the Executive Council of the American Federation of Labor has given us jurisdiction over sleeping car and dining car workers, as set forth in an action by the Council and reported by President Flore to our Twenty-first General Convention at Cleveland, Ohio, during the week of August 8-13, 1921, the following language appearing in the official record:

"Upon the application of the Hotel and Restaurant Employees International Alliance and Bartenders International League of America, it was decided that the following jurisdiction of that organization be recognized:

" 'Jurisdiction covering all hotel and restaurant employees in all branches and departments, excepting those engaged in mechanical work now organized under A. F. of L. and barbers, tailors, laundry workers, drivers and chauffeurs.

" 'Bartenders, beverage dispensers and soda fountain workers.

" 'Sleeping and parlor car employees (conductors excepted) dining car employees (cooks and waiters).

" 'Culinary workers and beverage dispensers on steamboats. It is not intended that this is to change conditions now existing; it is to cover mostly culinary workers and beverage dispensers on lake, river, pleasure and resort steamers.'

"It is fairly possible that President Flore may write you further in connection with this matter, but, inasmuch as he requested me to convey the information relative to the action of the General Executive Board of our International Union, this letter goes forward as per his request."

(At a later date the Executive Council extended that jurisdiction to cover conductors in the dining car service.)

We appeared before the Executive Council as requested by them and submitted oral arguments in addition to the written statement filed and under date of May 22, 1928, we were advised by President Green that he had extended an invitation to the Brotherhood of Sleeping Car Porters to affiliate with the Federation through our International Union and that they had declined that invitation.

At a later date an application for charter was again made to the American Federation of Labor, and the Executive Council requested the President of the Federation of Labor to take the matter up with our International Union to ascertain whether our position in the matter had changed and in a conference held at New Orleans at which Secretary-Treasurer Hesketh was present, we advised the President of the Federation that our position was not changed and that we still maintained our claim for jurisdiction over sleeping car porters. The President gave his assurance that the Council would take no action without our International Union being heard on the subject. This assurance, however, was not made good. Without any knowledge that the Executive Council was to take action, the following press dispatch reached us from Miami, Florida, where the Executive Council was in session in February, 1929:

"It was decided to issue Federal Union charters to Pullman porters, the objections of President Flore of the hotel and restaurant employees having been considered sufficiently meritorious to prevent issuance of a national charter. It is estimated that between 4,000 and 6,000 are now in the independent organization. Negotiations will be carried on with the head of this organization regarding issuance of local charters."

"On February 28, 1928, we were further advised from President Green that it was the opinion of the Executive Council that it could not grant the application (of the Brotherhood of Sleeping Car Porters) for an international charter of affiliation but that they would grant them local union or Federal charters, affiliating them direct to the American Federation of Labor.

In response to that information we filed the following claim with the American Federation of Labor:

> The Executive Council of the American Federation of Labor under the leadership of the late Mr. Samuel Gompers have definitely granted to the Hotel and Restaurant Employees International Alliance and Bartenders International League of America jurisdiction over sleeping car porters, we maintain that the decision of the Executive Council of the American Federation of Labor still stands and that any Federal labor union or local union of sleeping car porters chartered under the American Federation of Labor through the decision of the Miami meeting or otherwise, will be the property of the Hotel and Restaurant Employees International League of America and we shall so claim and maintain."

At the last convention of the A. F. of L., locals of the sleeping car porters were represented for the first time and Local No. 18068 of New York submitted Resolution No. 54 urging trade union educational and organization campaigns among Negro workers, which resolution was referred to the Committee on Organization, and favorably reported to the convention.

The Black Worker, the official organ of the Brotherhood of Sleeping Car Porters, is published on the 1st and 15th of each month.[1]

INDEPENDENT NEGRO UNIONS

With the exception of two major occupational groupings wherein Negro workers maintain a complete monopoly, as the Pullman porters and dining car waiters, the organization of Negro unions has been a protest against the attitude of white organized labor in the United States toward Negro workers. When out of the unions Negroes complained against the exclusion policies of these organizations. When these Negro workers are permitted to join they complain of racial prejudice within the unions. The growth of the collective bargaining movement among these workers along with the adverse situations presented by the or-

---

[1]The American Federation of Labor does not officially recognize the Brotherhood of Sleeping Car Porters. Each unit of porters is known to the Federation as an integral Local Union of Sleeping Car Porters.

ganized labor groups gave rise to the organization of these independent Negro groups. In many cases they have been only local organizations as the sheet metal workers in Charleston, S. C., the plumbers, the lathers and the electricians in Chicago, Ill., the asphalt workers in Milwaukee, Wis. Other groups have organized nationally and have evolved a bargaining power that has been of immense value to the workers concerned. In the independent transportation unions of Negro workers, the Negro employees have found organization the only way to hold such opportunities as they had on the railroads.

Less than ten years ago the agitation for the formation of Negro unions had reached the point where a United Negro Trades* was suggested. Such an organization would create and stimulate the Negro worker and would encourage, advocate and foster the formation of independent Negro unions when the white unions deny Negro workers a union card. The United Negro Trades would be to the Negro worker "what the United Hebrew Trades and the Italian Chamber of Commerce are to the Jewish and Italian workers, respectively." The plan did not get beyond this initial presentation.

The following data are presented on the foremost independent groups:

The ASSOCIATION OF TRAIN PORTERS, BRAKEMEN AND SWITCHMEN was organized at Florence, S. C., in July, 1918, by 18 porters. It was then called the Colored Organization of Railway Trainmen. On December 2, 1919 it incorporated under the laws of Virginia under the present name with the right to organize and establish locals or branches generally throughout the United States.* The field for such an organization was great. The large number of Negro employees on southern railroads had no organization through which their grievances might be expressed.

Some of the principles for which the association stands are:

1—The right to organize.

2—The right of employees to be consulted prior to a decision of management adversely affecting their wages or work conditions.

3—No employee should be disciplined without a fair hearing by a designated officer of the carrier.

---

* New York Call, July 7, 1923, quoting the Messenger Magazine.
* Handbook of American Trade Unions, p. 89.

4—Proper classification of employees and reasonable definition of work hours.

5—Regularity of hours.

6—The principles of seniority.

The objects of the Association are: "To organize, develop, and improve the condition of the colored trainmen of America, to secure just and fair compensation for services rendered, and maintenance of proper wages together with fair working conditions for its members."

The Association has a membership of 1,700 colored train porters, brakemen and switchmen in 15 local lodges. In 1926 there were 28 local lodges. The present territorial jurisdiction covers 12 railroads in the South. The 15 local lodges are distributed as follows: Alabama, 2; District of Columbia, 1; Florida, 1; Georgia, 2; Louisiana, 1; Mississippi, 1; North Carolina, 2; South Carolina, 2; Tennessee, 2; Virginia, 1.

The ASSOCIATION OF COLORED RAILWAY TRAINMEN was organized at Knoxville, Tenn., in 1912 and was reorganized in 1918. Its purpose is stated as follows:

"To unite the colored railway employees, to extend their interests and promote their general welfare, to provide, aid and assistance to their families, to use legitimate and lawful means of harmonizing and rectifying differences between members of the association and employers."

The trade jurisdiction covers railway brakemen, switchmen and train porters. Funeral benefits are given to members.

In 1926 this organization had 4,800 members distributed in 60 locals, but in 1928 the membership had dropped to 3,000 with the same number of locals. These locals were distributed as follows: Alabama, 6; Arkansas, 2; Colorado, 2; Florida, 2; Georgia, 3; Illinois, 1; North Carolina, 4; South Carolina, 4; Tennessee, 7; Texas, 6; Virginia, 4; West Virginia, 2. One feature of its membership qualification is that:

"The organization will accept for membership men minus one arm or one leg as long as they are railway employees in such capacity as switch tender, baggage room porter, crossing flagmen, or call boy, and they must be ex-railway brakemen, switchmen or train porters."

The NATIONAL ALLIANCE OF POSTAL EMPLOYEES was organized at Chattanooga, Tennessee in 1913, by the colored employees of the railway mail service who, because of their race, were not eligible to membership in the Railway Mail Association. In 1923 the membership scope was extended to include all colored workers in the United States Postal Service.

The object of the Alliance is "to provide close relationship among postal employees to enable them to perfect any movement that will be for their benefit as a class and for the benefit of the Postal Service; also to conduct business for a fraternal beneficiary organization for the sole benefit of its members and their beneficiaries and make provision for the payment of benefits to them in case of death, temporary or permanent disability as a result of accident."

The government of the organization rests in an Executive Committee composed of nine district presidents and the general officers of the organization; namely, president, vice-president, secretary-treasurer, editor and auditor. The president is the executive head.

Membership qualifications are restricted to "any regular employee or certified substitute in the Post Office Department under civil service rules."

The organization grants death benefits and maintains a contributory disability and accident insurance.

In 1926 the membership of the National Alliance of Postal Employees was 1,700, distributed in 53 locals located in 25 states. In 1928 there were 3,300 members in 72 locals as follows: Alabama, 2; Arkansas, 2; California, 3; District of Columbia, 1; Florida, 2; Georgia, 10; Illinois, 3; Indiana, 1; Kansas, 1; Kentucky, 2; Louisiana, 2; Maryland, 2; Michigan, 1; Mississippi, 4; Missouri, 3; Nebraska, 1; New York, 1; North Carolina, 1; Ohio, 5; Pennsylvania, 2; South Carolina, 3; Tennessee, 5; Texas, 9; Virginia, 6.

The President of the Brotherhood of Dining Car Employees analyzes the scope and activity of that organization as follows:

"The total number of dining cars and terminal restaurant employees is about 10,400. Of this number about 7,000 are Negroes and 4,000 of them are employed in the present jurisdiction of the Brotherhood of Dining Car Employees. Approximately 3,000 of this number are members of the organization.*

---

* On January 15, 1930, President Lemus stated that the membership was 2800.

"The Brotherhood of Dining Car Employees studiously avoids propaganda. Moreover, despite the fact that more than two millions of dollars have been added to the compensation of dining car cooks-waiters in our organization sphere since 1921 solely because of the organization, we do not let the public in on it. Some of the waiters who got $57 per month on May 1, 1924, have got $70 since that date by virtue of the operation of a Brotherhood of Dining Car Employees' contract. Certainly it doesn't help any for those from whom we expect so-called "tips" to hear about it.

"This organization made the representations which got the then hitherto unheard or undreamed of 240 hour month and overtime compensation from the late Railroad Administration for *all* dining car cooks-waiters, and preserved them for its members with contracts on all carriers whose employees are our members, and indirectly for most of the craft.

"Each carrier operates its dining service under general supervision of the Vice-President in charge of Traffic or Transportation, with a Dining Car Superintendent in charge. All such are employees of the railroads whose patrons they serve. Here in Washington, our membership requires dealings with three different, distinct "sovereign" managements, viz., Atlantic Coast Line, (reactionary) Seaboard Air Line.

"At New York we deal with two managements: Pennsylvania for which there is no law of God nor man North (or South) of 53; New York Central (very liberal; meets us as equals).

"At Boston we deal with three—Boston and Albany (liberal and argumentative); Boston and Maine (jewel); "New Haven" (technical but respectably so; very argumentative.) By all of them I am recognized as representative and admitted to conference. The Southern has been so liberal in dealing with me as representative until one of the employees and members of the Organization has circulated report that I am a "stool pigeon" for that carrier management.

"Norfolk and Western folk are liberal and Baltimore and Ohio management virtually considers its employees members of the Organization. I am waiting for them to get it into their heads that this is a Brotherhood, not a machine to get increases in pay and improved working rules, only to have them drop out after the accomplishment.

TABLE XIII

INDEPENDENT NEGRO UNIONS

	NUMBER OF LOCALS	MEMBERSHIP
National Alliance of Postal Employees	72	3,300
Association of Colored Railway Trainmen	60	3,000
Brotherhood of Dining Car Employees	9	2,800
Association of Train Porters, Brakemen and Switchmen	15	1,700
Waiters Beneficial Association (Philadelphia)	—	275
Brotherhood of Dining & Sleeping Car Employees[1]	—	260
Electricians Union (Chicago)[2]	—	200
Plumbers Union (Chicago)[2]	—	200
Plasterers Union (Chicago)[2]	—	200
Waiters' Exchange No. 836 (Baltimore)	—	175
Junior Wood, Wire and Metal Lathers (Chicago)[3]	—	150
Red Cap and Railway Employees Association (Phila.)	—	150
Ship Workers' Beneficial Association (Pensacola, Fla.)	—	100
Sheet Metal Workers (Charleston, S. C., Savannah, Ga.)[4]	—	75
Asphalt Workers (Milwaukee)	—	Not given
Railway Men's Benevolent Protective Association (Chicago)	—	Not given
Train Porters and Brakemen (St. Louis)	—	Not given
International Order of Colored Locomotive Firemen (Savannah, Ga.)	—	Not given
Independent Hod Carriers' Union (Birmingham, Ala.)	—	Not given
Total Membership		12,585

"We build as we go. The other fellow must appreciate our work, as the B. and O. men do. We do not waste the money of the faithful trying to get the other fellow, and, under no circumstances will this Administration accept one mill to finance organization campaigns. We are teaching the practical meaning of 'Not alms but opportunity'. Not a penny from philanthropy to keep up this Organization. Let what little philanthropic support is available be kept where it belongs."

---

[1] Harris, Abram L., states in "The Negro in the American Labor Movement," Harris and Spero, that this union operates chiefly on the Great Northern Railroad and includes white cooks employed on the Soo Line.

[2] Adapted from "The Negro Industrial Proletariat," James Ford. Trade Union Educational League of America, p. 19.

[3] Vide: "Chicago" p. 174.

[4] Vide: "Sheet Metal Workers," p. 80.

"We have 9 locals. Territory: Boston to Jacksonville; Atlanta to New Orleans; Charleston, S. C., to Pittsburgh."

The RAILWAY MEN'S INTERNATIONAL BENEVOLENT INDUSTRIAL ASSOCIATION was organized in May 12, 1915 as a protest organization because of the exclusion of Negroes by the railway brotherhoods and certain unions in the railway department of the American Federation of Labor. It is classified as a "labor union open to all Negro railway employees". In 1920 this organization had 1150 financial members and 17 locals in Chicago. Though capably managed and well advised by Negro professional men, the membership of this union has since declined because the President felt, according to the *Messenger* for March, 1926,— "that he could make a score or more of different crafts of workers function in one organization, just as a chef makes a half dozen or more soups in one pot".

It is the opinion of the organizer of the Association that there were several high points in its activity. This opinion is presented in the following statement:

"In 1924 with 187 men out of 10,500 who paid $1.65 each, plus $100 contributed by four pulman porters and myself, we moved for an increase in pay, the 240 hour month, pay for preparatory time, and the right of the men to be represented by men of their choice and other considerations.

"Before we could make preliminary application for hearing to the U. S. Railroad Labor Board at Chicago, the company held an election and twenty odd district representatives selected by the men signed and made effective (then and now) the Employee Representative Plan and gave a million dollars a year more in pay. The climax came when certain well known "race leaders" framed me, had me arrested and wired a vicious statement to over one hundred colored newspapers. But we got the million dollars increase for less than $500 spent.

"From a membership in October, 1917, of less than 100 the Railway Men's International Benevolent Industrial went to a membership of better than 15,000 by 1920, embracing 187 locals, representing every grade of colored employee and establish on practically every railroad in the United States employing colored men. In Chicago the combined local membership represented 1,150 financial members about October 1919. In Savannah, Georgia, at the same time the membership was about 430. Chicago represented dining car men and Pullman porters with a few shopmen. Savannah represented engine, train service and shopmen exclusively. Boston and Pasadena, California, St. Paul and New Orleans were the other extremities.

"The high points were many. The greatest was when with less than 100 members in the country in February 1918 we appeared at Washington to call on President Wilson for representatives of railway workers, bluffed our way through if strength is considered and got before the Lane Commission the case of the Negro Railway Workers. That eliminated differential in pay and treatment and gave skilled Negro railway workers their first recognition other than the favor of some kindly disposed immediate or general official. Next, dining car and sleeping car men were at the same time given their first consideration as anything but "boys." On two other occasions at Washington these men were well represented if the fact that they were raised from $25 to $60 a month, with overtime rates on the mileage basis after 11,000 miles per calendar month. Also, these were the first and only occasions when the dining car officials and the Pullman officers were compelled to sit across the table and meet the demands of the men. It is apparent the men won. They still enjoy rates equal to or higher than these rates.

"Cold nerve was required when our representatives sat in on the great Labor Board hearing at Chicago when the Nationl Agreements granted during government control were sought to be kept in effect by the so-called standard railway brotherhoods (white). We knew this would have been a labor monopoly from which Negroes would ultimately suffer because of jurisdictional supremacy by these unions. The record shows we asked flatly that the national agreements be abolished and annuled and that no wage or working condition conference be called or legal unless all men subject to the results of same be represented at the conference and allowed to vote.

"At present the Negro employees are not sufficiently organized to give themselves the needed protection through concerted protest. However, the desire to organize is growing and the type of men who are taking the leadership in widely separated communities is a high class, educated type. The request for organization comes from the men because the same problem is there in so far as the desire of the whites to displace them is concerned. Frankly the men are not used to organized effort of this kind and the final results will depend absolutely on the local leadership, propaganda, favorable action by influential outsiders of the labor and capital groups and a single heading up organization." *

In its hey-day the organization protested against "unfair and bad" working conditions of the employer and against unfair practices on the part of the American Federation of Labor and the railway brotherhoods.

The COLORED PROJECTIONISTS ASSOCIATION OF BALTIMORE is an independent organization organized in 1917. At its incipiency, vigorous efforts were made to become identified with the Baltimore local of the International Association of Stage and Theatrical Employees and Motion Picture Machine Operators. These efforts, which included an appeal to the American Federation of Labor, were to no avail and since that time the union has decided to remain independent. These operators work only in theatres catering exclusively to colored people.

The WAITERS BENEFICIAL ASSOCIATION OF PHILADELPHIA, PENNSYLVANIA, was organized in 1903 and was chartered in 1907. In January 1928 it had a membership of 275. Because Negro waiters used to have a monopoly on that occupation in the past is said to account for the separate Negro organization mainly, and tradition has operated to keep it a separate one.

The REDCAP AND RAILROAD EMPLOYEES ASSOCIATION OF PHILADELPHIA is an independent Negro union maintaining an international charter. It was organized in 1921 and claimed in January 1928 a membership of 150. The fact that this union is exclusively Negro is due to the employment of none other than Negro workers as Redcaps and Station Cleaners in Philadelphia.

The SHIP WORKERS BENEFICIAL ASSOCIATION No. 2 OF PENSACOLA, FLORIDA, was organized in 1923. It has no affiliation with the International Longshoremen's Association or the American Federation of Labor. It claims a total membership of 100 Negro workers. The work conditions, and the scarcity of work have prevented the growth of solidarity within this group.

WAITERS' EXCHANGE No. 836 was organized in Baltimore, Maryland, in 1916. It has a membership of 175. Practically all

---

* Correspondence, R. L. Mays, December 5, 1929.

of the waiting in Baltimore is done by colored men, though the headwaiters and chefs are white. It appears that this exchange was formerly affiliated to the American Federation of Labor, but withdrew after a jurisdictional dispute with the Seamen's Union in 1922 and 1923. The question arose over the use of colored waiters on two steamers in 1922 and 1923. In this controversy the A. F. of L. refused to aid the waiters' exchange, and, therefore, the waiters withdrew from the Federation and became an independent union.[1]

The colored firemen employed on the Frisco, Illinois Central and the Louisiana and Arkansas Railroads are now being organized into a union known as the INTERSTATE ORDER OF COLORED LOCOMOTIVE FIREMEN AND ENGINEERS.

THE AMERICAN NEGRO LABOR CONGRESS

Except for the activities of the Industrial Workers of the World and the Communist vehicle, "The American Negro Labor Congress,"[2] militancy in the advocacy of Negro membership in trade unions has not been a forte of organized labor in America. The Conference for Progressive Labor Action does promise to exert a favorable influence in this direction. The Communist movement, however, succeeded in arousing more public interest and editorial comment on organizing Negro labor than has ever appeared in the public press. Though the movement has done little work in the actual organization of Negroes, it is interesting to note that when it started some of the reactionary labor organizations unwittingly gave this group their unqualified support. Letters of encouragement were received from Central Labor bodies, State Federations and National Unions. In thirty letters received by the Congress in answer to a request for information on Negro membership, only two officials sought to learn more about the movement before giving the information.

---

[1] The investigator reports "this is the second colored working group which I have found to have had some trouble with the A. F. of L. or an international union regarding justice for organized workers. The other group was in Philadelphia and concerned a jurisdictional dispute arising between local No. 420 and local No. 63 of the Hod Carriers Union. In this particular instance the International Hod Carriers, Building and Common Laborers Union refused to interfere in the controversy and protect Local No. 420—all of the members of which are colored—in maintaining its rights.

[2] Not to be confused with the National Negro Labor Congress called by the Brotherhood of Sleeping Car Porters for January 26-31, 1930. at Chicago.

When it did become known that the Congress was "un-American," oral and written protests were profuse. The Chicago Federation of Labor issued a four page circular letter under date of July 18, 1925 stating in part that "the purpose of the Communists, or their professed interest in the Negro worker, is not to organize him where he properly belongs, viz.; into unions affiliated to the American Federation of Labor, but to exploit him as a means of creating turmoil and dissension in any local where they can inject their program. *The American Federationist* spoke editorially against such a movement for Negro workers for whom they (The A. F. of L.) felt morally responsible. While the Communists issued their propaganda through the Negro Champion ("militant organ of the Negro masses") and the *Daily Worker,* the white daily press was bestirred to counteract such a movement through its editorial columns. The activities of the Communists in organizing Negro workers did not affect Philadelphia Negroes, according to the *Philadelphia Bulletin.*[1] The *Grand Rapids* (Mich.) *Press* did not see how black and red would mix.[2] *The Augusta* (Me.) *Journal* felt that the Negroes would be disposed to stand with their benefactors.[3] Police Commissioner Turley of Dallas, Tex., declared that Communism would not find a fertile field among the Negroes of Texas.[4] To the *Galveston News* the Communist effort was insignificant because "it excited so little attention.[5] *The Watertown* (N. Y.) *Times* believed the Negro would remain unchanged when the Congress had adjourned.[6] The *Philadelphia Bulletin* claimed that the Negro disposition was too happy a one to join that army of discontented.[7]. The *Christian Science Monitor* saw no hope in a movement whose tenets taught class hatred or racial consciousness.[8] *The Saint Louis Globe-Democrat* was gratified to see organized labor fight the movements.[9] The *Saint Louis Times* saw no danger in Russian agitators corrupting the loyalty of "our Negroes."[10] "The Negroes of the United States are not so foolish as to exchange an American twenty-dollar gold piece for what would be less than the equivalent of one-dollar in Russian paper money," claimed the *Memphis* (Tenn.) *Commercial Appeal.*[11]

[1] Editorial, October 27, 1925.
[2] August 25, 1925.
[3] August 12, 1925.
[4] August 18, 1925.
[5] November 3, 1925.
[6] August 13, 1925.

[7] August 11, 1925.
[8] August 11, 1925.
[9] September 6, 1925.
[10] November 4, 1925.
[11] October 26, 1925.

Nevertheless the congress was called and 40 Negro delegates, representing unorganized and organized groups of workers were present. Violent denunciations of the present economic order, and fiery criticisms of the American racial hierarchy were given. Beyond that the congress bore no fruit. Another congress has been called for St. Louis in May 1920.

The platform of the American Negro Labor Congress is stated as—

1—The organization of all Negro and white workers into industrial unions.

2—The emancipation of Negro farmers and agricultural laborers.

3—Abolition of "Jim Crowism" and social restrictions.

4—Removal of all restrictions against Negroes in the military service.

5—Abolition of segregation and high rents.

6—Equal school facilities for Negro and white children.

7—Removal of political disfranchisement.

8—Removal of discrimination in the courts.

9—Organization of Negro masses against imperialism.

The organization favors that "all Labor Unions shall affiliate with the American Federation of Labor wherever this is reasonably possible and create a large unity of labor.[1] The membership of its local councils shall be of delegates from Negro labor unions, mixed labor unions, organized Negro industrial workers, organized Negro agricultural workers, delegates elected by three or more Negro workers who work together in a workshop, factory or farm.

The Negro Champion is the official organ of the American Negro Labor Congress, and it is the duty of every member to subscribe to that organ.

Further evidence of the activity of the left-wing labor groups is the fact that there are approximately 1,500 Negro members of national leagues and unions affiliated to the Trade Union Unity League. In addition to this number, J. W. Ford, Director of the Negro Department of the TUUL estimates that there are about 1,000 Negro workers in district groups not yet separated into national unions. The Negro membership is distributed as follows:

National Miners Union	500
Needle Trades Industrial Union	500
Marine Workers League	300
Railroad Workers Industrial League	200

---

[1] Constitution and Program of the American Negro Labor Congress, p. 8.

No records were available from the National Textile Union, but Robert W. Dunn, Executive Director of the Labor Research Association estimates the Negro membership "somewhere between 25 and 50."

At a recently organized national unemployment council held in New York under the auspices of the TUUL there were 48 Negro delegates among the 200 attending. Five of the thirteen members of the council's national committee were Negroes.

There are 25 Negro officials in the various unions, leagues and district executive committees of the unions and leagues.

NEGROES AND ORGANIZED LABOR IN SELECTED CITIES

NEW YORK, N. Y.

As early as 1906 there were more than 1385 members of trade unions in New York. The distribution of these workers in 1906 and 1910, as found by Mary White Ovington was as follows:

	1906	1910
Asphalt Workers	320	350
Teamsters	300	400
Rock Drillers and Tool Sharpeners	250	240
Cigar Makers	121	165
Bricklayers	90[1]	21
Waiters	90	Not obtained
Carpenters	60	40
Plasterers	45	19
Double Drum Hoisters	30	37
Safety and Portable Engineers	26	35
Eccentric Firemen	15	0
Letter Carriers	10	30
Pressmen	10	Not obtained
Printers	6	8
Butchers	3	3
Lathers	3	7
Painters	3	Not obtained
Coopers	1	2
Sheet Metal Workers	1	1
Rockmen	1	Not obtained
Total	1,385	1,358

[1] The large number of bricklayers in 1906 is questioned by the man, himself a bricklayer, who made the second count. However, the number greatly decreased in 1908 when the stagnation in business compelled many men to seek work in other cities.

Mainly because of the increased employment in longshore work, building labor and subway construction the number of organized workers had reached a peak of approximately 12,000 in 1926. Other organizations contributing to the increase were the plasters, the cement finishers, letter carriers, post office clerks, federal employees, musicians, garment workers, hod carriers, and teamsters and chauffeurs. The locals of those internationals denying membership to Negro workers follow those policies as rigidly in New York as elsewhere. In many instances, however, the power exercised by craft groups of Negro workers has forced the unions to agree to the demands of that group of workers. The Motion Picture Machine Operators Union No. 306 is an example of such a situation.*

Because of the many problems faced in organizing Negro workers a committee sponsored by the New York Urban League spent many months during the early part of 1925 ascertaining the attitude of unions toward admitting Negroes. On May 23, 1925 over 25 local and international unions were represented at a conference on the subject. This conference created the "Trade Union Committee for Organizing Negro Workers". This organization hoped to do for Negro workers "what the Women's Trade Union League does for women workers". It hoped, not only to organize Negro workers, but to secure justice for them inside the unions, and "to educate both Negro and white workers toward a realization of their common economic interest."

The American Fund for Public Service provided a sum of money to start the enterprise, but current expenses were paid by contributions from the local unions of the city. To secure these funds the executive secretary addressed union meetings, "practically every night". In so doing, of course, he was carrying out the aim of the Committee to educate white workers in their common economic interest with Negro workers, but little time was left for organizing the Negro workers themselves. The Committee received considerable publicity, and with only the encouragement of impersonal newspaper stories, some Negro workers came to the headquarters asking to be introduced to the unions of their craft. One man wrote a letter to the Committee asking that he and a group of fourteen associates from various occupations be visited and led into their respective trade unions. A baker wrote from Newport News, Va., to see whether

---

* See Amusements.

the committee could help him join a union. Perhaps fifteen or twenty Negro men and women were inducted into the following unions: The Ladies Garment Workers Union, the Carpenters Union, the Laundry Workers Union, the Teamsters Union, the Bookkeepers and Stenographers Union, the Painters Union, the Iron Workers Union, the Common Laborers Union, and the Furriers Union in the first five months of the committee's activity. Work was also begun with the 16,000 colored laundry workers. A free employment bureau was opened, publicity was issued through the motion picture houses, and the cooperation of Negro ministers sought.

The executive board of the Trade Union Committee for Organizing Negro Workers consisted of six white and five colored unionists from the following unions: elevator operators, bookkeepers and stenographers, teamsters, carpenters, subway and tunnel operators, ladies garment workers, teachers, tobacco workers and laundry workers. The chairman of the committees is first vice-president of the New York State Federation of Labor and in charge of the New York Compensation Bureau of the Building Trades.

When the Brotherhood of Sleeping Car Porters started its extensive organization scheme, the executive secretary became an organizer for that group. Thus the movement died before it had been able to achieve any outstanding results. One cause of its decline was the fact that the trade unions did not make the financial contributions to the work that they promised.

Within recent years the most extensive organization efforts other than that of the Pullman porters, have been exerted among the public laundry workers. The movement has had little or no success so far as the unskilled and semi-skilled Negro worker is concerned. The present effort of the International Ladies Garment Workers Union in organizing the 4,000 Negro women employed under its jurisdiction promises to show immediate results.

Because Negro workers are admitted into mixed locals, and because of the opportunities these workers have had to participate jointly in the many strikes and disputes that have occurred within the city, it is apparent that these workers have a greater understanding of the tenets and values of collective bargaining than is found in many other cities.

There are approximately 10,000 Negro members of trades unions in Chicago. In 1919-1920 the Chicago Commitee on Race Relations found 12,106 Negro members. The proportion of organized Negro workers to the Chicago Negro population at that time was almost exactly the same as the proportion of white members to the white population.

Negroes are members in large numbers of the hod carriers and the musicians unions. The building trades organizations, particularly the carpenters, masons and plasters, and the teamsters and chauffeurs unions have Negro memberships of considerable size. In all unions admitting Negro workers the organization was in a mixed local except in the case of the painters union, and the hotel and restaurant employees where separate locals are maintained; and in the blacksmiths union where the national policy of admitting Negro workers to auxiliary locals is followed.

Two unions having large Negro memberships in 1920, the Stock Yards Uunion—particularly Local No. 651, and the Flat Janitors Union have weakened during the decade and forfeited the control once wielded.

Following the Chicago race riots in 1919 the labor unions of that city were particularly active in the organization of Negro workers. Many of them placed Negro organizers on the field who were able to enroll large numbers of Negro members. The experience of the Stock Yards' strike of 1904 when Negroes were used as strikebreakers had proved an invaluable lesson and the then (1920) active Amalgamated Meat Cutters and Butcher Workmen's Union of North America welcomed Negroes to any of the 40 locals they wished to join. The 1918-1919 issue of the Negro Year Book reported 60 per cent of the Negro workers in this industry as organized. Three paid Negro organizers were maintained.

The painters' unions of Chicago followed the organization method used by that organization in other sections of the country by organizing Negroes into separate locals. The incident is related as follows. *

"During July 1920, 20 Negro painters applied to the Painters District Council for membership in the painters

* The Negro in Chicago—p. 417-418.

union. They passed the required examination, but, instead of being placed in the existing painters union, were given temporary working permits which identified them as members of the SOUTH SIDE COLORED LOCAL. They immediately suspected that some effort was being made to place them in a separate Negro local in which they could not get the full union membership. They returned to the President of the District Council who explained that he had to keep track of all temporary permits issued, and inasmuch as the charter for their local was not yet issued he could not know the number until issued. He had to put the description on the cards to identify the men temporarily.

"A charter for the local was given from national headquarters, and the new cards were issued, designating them simply as members of Local No. ———. The membership of this local, exclusively Negro, grew from 20 to 75 in two months. One of the Negro officials of the local stated that its members had been working in all parts of the Chicago District, including the North Side and Evanston, and that they had representation on the District Council. The attitude of the white workers, he states, was a little cool on the first day, but there is now no evidence of friction. He thought that the members of this local were well pleased and happy."

Other unions reporting Negro members were thee organizations of bakers, steam and operating engineers, government workers, clothing workers, typographical workers, firemen and oilers, seamen, barbers, public health nurses, teachers, well diggers and the yardsmen and coal hikers.

The Electrical Workers Local No. 134 admitted its first Negro member on six months probation in December 1928. This Negro electrician has sought membership in the union for several years. Though a master electrician he had been "pulled off" several jobs because he was a non-union worker.

A Negro master plumber has tried for several years to enter the Journeymen Plumbers Union. This worker is reported as having passed the examination given though the officials told him he had failed. He was also rejected because two plumbers would not vouch for him. Because his work has been bombed several times it is now difficult for him to secure employment.

In other instances the Negro worker has been told in no uncertain terms that it is to his advantage to join the union.

In the case of one powerful local union bombs had served to convince at least one Negro worker that his safety lay in organization. Practically no discrimination exists in this union "due to the education members receive," writes the secretary of that local.

Only such Negro barbers as cater to white trade receive the full benfits of union membership. Though a number of Negro barbers are members of the Chicago Barbers' Union, many of that number work at a scale lower than that set by the union.

In 1920 colored waiters broke a strike of the Hotel and Restaurant Employees union in six of the city's principal hotels. They continue to hold these jobs as non-union workers. Within recent years, however, it has been possible to organize the Negro cabaret waiters of the South Side. In 1926 this union (Local No. 444) had 150 members.

Indicative of how national rulings regarding Negro membership apply to local situations is shown in a statement by the local chairman of Lodge No. 2219 of the Brotherhood of Railway Clerks. This organization, as well as the organization of Express Workers, does not admit Negroes. The chairman writes:

"I am employed at the Illinois Central Depot at Chicago, Ill., and come in contact day and night with at least fifty or more colored men employed by that company—the American Railway Express Company. These Negroes are all good men. I am personally acquainted with them, but cannot organize them because of our by-laws, and colored men will not take a separate charter. I think as a worker for organized labor something should be done for these colored men. Our system should be changed to include these Negroes or some representatives sent here to organize them."

Indicative of the many difficulties faced by Negro workers is the problem presented by the Local No. 74 of the International Wood, Wire and Metal Lathers Union of Chicago, which refused to admit Negro members and furthermore was accused of intimidating such Negro workers as attempted to follow that craft in the city.

During August 1929 a representative of the U. S. Department of Labor attempted to effect a conciliation between the two groups. The story of the situation is reported as follows:*

---

* Vide: Chicago Defender, August 10, 1929.

"The Junior National Wood, Wire and Metal Lathers Union was formed in 1925 after repeated requests for admittance in to No. 74 were met with rebuffs.

The Chicago local of the international, in violation of the law of the parent body, it was stated, refused to admit Negro members. It is definitely stated in the constitution that no one shall be refused membership into the union because of race, creed or color.

Jesse Menefee, business manager for the union and spokesman for the committee, told in detail the grievances of the men. He pointed out that they had ceased to persist in efforts to be recognized by the international body, but merely desired to be left alone to work in peace on the jobs wihch they secured. Business agents of Local No. 74 have used every conceivable method of intimidation to drive them out of the lathing business, the speaker said. The situation is on the verge of open warfare, and it is because of this that they are asking the Department of Labor to help, he concluded—

"When the representatives of Local No. 74 are unable to drive our men off jobs, and fail to induce the owners of the jobs to take us off, they resort to unlawful practices," Menefee declared.

It was revealed that all the appeals that had been made to the American Federation of Labor, parent body of the international, have been referred to the latter's national office at Cleveland. The Cleveland office, stating that the affair was strictly a local one, requested the correspondents to take up the matter with officials of the Chicago local. Local No. 74, it was said, refused to discuss the matter. Officials of that organization would not reply to letters or communicate with the Negro lathers in any respect. Speakers for the latter organization said:

"After numerous continuances throughout several months, Fred Wayman, busines agent of the International Lathers Union (white) and George T. Moore, members of the union, were arraigned before Judge Samuel Trude of the municipal court Tuesday morning on a charge of intimidation of colored workers and members of the Negro Lathers Union, and after several hours of legal clashes and arguments on both sides the men were found not guilty by the court.

It is alleged that for the past twenty-three years Negro workers have been molested by various trade unions, and many have been brought into court, according to the records, but almost in every case they were discharged.

Attorney Hammond, aiding the state in the prosecution, placed several members of the local on the witness stand, and they told how they had been threatened and warned to leave their jobs. Many of these men had children and have been unable to work for several months for fear of these terrorists.

Witnesses for the prosecution told how these men had visited the jobs on which they were working, threatening and warning them not to continue their work.

According to the evidence introduced by the state after the complaints had been sworn out against the defendants, they continued in their molestation of these lathers.

Judge William E. Helander of the racket court was first assigned to the case and after several continuances attorneys for the defendants asked for a change of venue on the grounds that the court was "prejudiced and partial". Judge Helander, in granting the change of venue stated, "That these men want a change of venue because I would not adhere to their demands". A change of venue was granted and the case assigned to Judge Samuel Trude.

Several months ago the circuit court of Cook county granted an injunction preventing the members of the International Lathers Union from interfering with the work of the colored union, but from all indications they are still being molested."

The Junior National Wood, Wire and Metal Lathers' Union has a membership of 150 Negro lathers.

PHILADELPHIA, PENNSYLVANIA.

There are 110 local unions in Philadelphia. The principal unions admiting Negroes are the locals of carpenters, longshoremen, musicians, hoisting engineers, brickmasons, hod carriers, laborers, teamsters and cement finishers. The total Negro union membership in Pennsylvania is 7,098, between 4,500 and 5,000 of whom are found in Philadelphia.

The largest group are members of the International Longshoremen's Association and number 1,500.[1] The next largest number is in locals of hod carriers, building and common laborers unions, and is estimated to be 1,200. The teamsters, the musicians, the paving cutters and the carpenters follow in the order named.

In occupations other than those aforementioned Negro membership is negligible. The plasterers with 80 members, the garment workers with 100 members cover the major portion of organized Negro workers. The carpenters have a Negro organizer but the other skilled trades make no active effort to secure Negro membership. In fact "the more intelligent Negroes will not accept appointment as organizers because in most cases they are expected either to join segregated locals or to urge Negro workmen to join segregated locals already formed.[2]

While on one hand difficulties in the organization and the maintenance of unions with Negroes have not obtained, on the other, Negro workers are not invited to join, as in the case of the Typographical Union No. 2 where a "cursory survey" supposedly showed that Negro and white printers had no common problems. This led not to conflict but to segregation. Today no Negroes are employed in composing rooms with whites.

PITTSBURGH, PENNSYLVANIA.

In 1925 there were only 518 Negroes in Pittsburgh who belonged to trades unions. Of this number 478 were members of building trades unions. The 200 miners living in the Hill District of the city were employed in non-union mines. Only one union, the wood and metal lathers had Negro apprentices. The plasterers do not admit Negroes to membership, nor did the plumbers. The bricklayers union permitted Negro membership but did not encourage it. The carpenters had a few Negro members of long standing, but made no effort to encourage a larger number. The electrical workers have made Negro membership virtually impossible.

The hod carriers, building and common laborers union and the union of cement finishers have the largest Negro memberships. The business agent of one of the hod carriers locals, a mixed local, is Negro and a former organizer of the A. F. of L.

---

[1] Forrester Washington in "The Negro Survey of Pennsylvania" (1925) gives the number of organized Negro longshoremen as 2,600. The figure given herein is 1928.

[2] Ibid.

Other unions not having Negro members were the elevator constructors, the sheet metal workers and the hoisting engineers.

The policy of the painters in organizing Negro workers into separate locals is defended by union officials on the following grounds:

1—Arguments between white and colored workers in the meetings often become personal and end with trouble.

2—After the Negro enters a mixed union he usually wants the distinction of being the only Negro in there and will not encourage others to join.

3—It is hard collecting dues from Negro workers.

4—Negroes "naturally" get second choice when men are being sent on a job.

5—Negroes violate union rules more frequently than whites.

The officials believe that a separate union will aid them in stabilizing the morale of the white group, and permit the weeding out of a major portion of the aforementioned problems of Negro membership.

Though the plumbers will not accept Negro workers there is one Negro master plumber in the city who is given union workmen whenever they are desired or are necessary. The opposition of this union to Italians and other foreign groups appeared to be as strong as that toward Negroes. *

BALTIMORE, MARYLAND.

In the National Urban League's study on "The Negro at Work in Baltimore", the union status of Negroes is reported as follows:

"It is a fact that in the 'open shops' there is an almost complete exclusion of Negroes from the skilled positions and many of the semi-skilled ones for which the unions are in no sense responsible; and in practically all of the independent crafts, such as carpentry, brick masonry, plumbing and steamfitting, there is almost total exclusion for which the employers are not responsible. For in the former case union organizations are not tolerated, and in the latter employers willing to use Negroes have been definitely prohibited by the unions."

---

* Vide: Harris, Abram L., The Negro Worker in Pittsburgh. Reid, Ira De A., The Negro in Major Industries and Building Trades of Pittsburg. National Urban League: "The Negro in the Hill District of Pittsburgh.

At the time of this investigation there were 114 locals affiliated with the Baltimore Federation of Labor. These locals divide themselves into three groups.

1—Those crafts in which Negroes are not employed.

2—Those crafts in which Negroes are employed but are not admitted into unions.

3—Those lines of work in which Negroes are employed and are permitted to organize in separate locals.

Group 1 covered 54 unions. Group 2 consisted of independent craft unions, carpenters, plumbers and steamfitters, painters and decorators, paperhangers and mechanics, all of which excluded Negroes from membership.

In the third group are locals in which Negroes have membership in separate locals. These unions were the longshoremen, hod carriers and common laborers, musicians, freight handlers and the federal employees. In 1923 this group had a membership of 1,980. In 1928 the total membership was 1,476.

Independent Negro labor organizations of hod carriers, building laborers and railway men having a membership of approximately 1,900 in 1923 were non-existent in 1928.

Labor unions on the whole have a good status and are recognized by business interests. Unionism is well established among longshoremen, carpenters, bricklayers, musicians, but are weak among garment workers.

Relations between white and colored workers seem to be fair on the whole. The two recent incidents bearing on labor-race relations in Baltimore are as follows:

1—In September, 1927, the organized white motion picture machine operators went on strike over the question of wages. The Negro independent operators furnished strikebreakers for the theatre owners. As soon as the theatre owners could they engaged white scabs to take colored operators' places. In the meantime, overtures had been made to get colored stage hands to organize and affiliate with the A. F. of L. The white operators were willing to help organize them. After the colored operators scabbed on the white striking operators, the latter lost interest in the colored stage hands and nothing has been done since on the proposition, nor can the Baltimore Federation of Labor do anything to heal the wound.

2—In 1922 and 1923 a dispute arose between the colored Waiters Exchange and the Seamen's Union relative to the use of colored waiters on two steamers. Colored waiters felt that they should share the waiting with the whites or be allowed to work on the two steamers. Appeals were made to the A. F. of L. in an attempt to adjust the matter. The A. F. of L. left the matter to the International, but nothing was done to appease the colored waiters. Becoming discouraged the Exchange waiters withdrew from the A. F. of L. and the International and have remained independent ever since. There has been no occasion for any trouble of this nature since, because colored waiters in Baltimore have a monopoly of the waiting work and never come into direct competition with white waiters. Custom and tacit agreement work in their favor.[1]

MINNEAPOLIS, MINNESOTA.

In 1925 there were 29 Negro members of the local unions of national organizations affiliated to the A. F. of L. Although the national constitutions of 40 local unions did not debar Negroes an account of race many of these unions found Negro membership impracticable or undesirable. Such appeared to be the case with the tile and marble setters helpers, the plumbers and the structural iron workers unions.

The 29 Negro trade unionists were distributed in unions as follows: Carpenters 1, Federal Employees 1, Milk Drivers 1, Musicians 6, Letter Carriers 5, Post Office Clerks 15. Negroes were formerly members of the bricklayers and masons union, the cigar makers, the firemen and oilers, the hotel and restaurant employees, the janitors, the molders, the paper hangers and the sheet metal workers unions.

The plumbers felt that white plumbers would not work with Negroes. The painters and paperhangers were "at present opposed to the admission of colored workers." The United Garment Workers were ready to admit Negro workers on a basis of equality.[2]

DAYTON, OHIO.

There are 48 trades unions in Dayton, 38 of which are affiliated with the Central Labor Union. Negro workers to the number of 350 are members of these unions, the largest number, 200, being members of the hod carriers, building and common laborers union. No Negroes are members of the plumbers,

---

[1] Vide: The Negro at Work in Baltimore, National Urban League.
[2] Vide: The Negro Population in Minneapolis. Harris, Abram L., 1925, p. 36-42.

machinists and the iron workers unions. The garment workers, tobacco workers, and building service employees are reported as having a few Negroes. The roofers union has 8 colored members. The Negro musicians have a separate union with 25 members. At one time 150 musicians were members of this body.

FORT WAYNE, INDIANA.

Although there are several strong unions in Fort Wayne, it is considered an open shop town. The largest number of Negroes (5) in any local belonged to the hod carriers union. One Negro is a member of the plasterers local. Negroes are barred from membership in the Amalgamated group in the rolling mills. At one time an attempt was made to organize a federal union of Negroes and a meeting for this purpose was held at a local church, but as the workers showed little interest the effort died aborning. *

LOS ANGELES, CALIFORNIA.

The official Year Book of Organized Labor for 1925 listed 106 local unions in Los Angeles with a membership of approximately 40,000. Most of these organized workers are out of the fields of work in which Negroes are engaged in large numbers. A total of 23 locals in industries where Negroes might be expected to be employed gives the membership of these locals as follows:

NAME OF UNION	MEMBERSHIP TOTAL	MEMBERSHIP NEGRO
Abbatoir Workers	1,000	7
Asbestos Workers	81	0
Barbers	500	0
Building Laborers	50	0
Bricklayers	1,100	80
Carpenters (Local A)	7,000	2
Carpenters (Local B)	1,100	1
Carpenters (Local C)	100	0
Cleaners and Dyers	300	15
Engineers, Hoisting	Not given	0
Flour and Cereal Workers	26	0
Hod Carriers	500	100
Iron Workers	250	0
Letter Carriers	1,000	50
Meat Cutters	300	0
Molders	600	0
Moving Picture Projectionists	Several hundred	0
Painters (District Council)	900	0
Musicians (Negro Local)	—	150
Plasterers	900	3
Post Office Laborers	40	18
Teamsters and Truck Drivers	300	0
Waiters	1,000	250

* Vide: A Survey of the Negro Population of Fort Wayne. National Urban League.

The table lists a total of 676 Negro members, about two-thirds of them waiters and musicians. The Negro letter carriers are completely organized. Although there are 500 hod carriers in the union, including 100 Negroes, it is not considered a well-organized trade in Los Angeles.

An inquiry into the lack of Negro members in the 12 locals reporting none reveals the following reported reasons:

ASBESTOS WORKERS—No Negroes in the trade; they cannot stand the heat.

BARBERS—White members insist upon separate locals for Negro barbers.

BUILDING LABORERS—Employers refuse to take Negroes.

HOISTING ENGINEERS—No Negroes in the trade; it is too dangerous.

FLOUR AND CEREAL WORKERS—No Negroes in the trade.

IRON WORKERS—Negroes would be taken if they followed the trade.

MEAT CUTTERS—There are only two (Negro) meat cutters in Los Angeles, who will join as soon as the matter is adjusted.

MOLDERS—Negroes do not belong to the trade.

MOTION PICTURE PROJECTIONISTS—Negroes are not important in this trade.

PAINTERS—There are not many skilled painters among Negroes.

TEAMSTERS AND TRUCK DRIVERS—Negro leaders are in the pay of large companies and refuse to let Negroes join.

A queer situation appears in the case of the painters. White contractors prefer white painters "because they want to keep unemployment among their own race as low as possible". Negro contractors prefer white painters "probably because the Negroes prefer to work with whites. Negro contractors have no trouble getting white painters to work for them".

The teamsters and truck drivers have made many attempts to interest Negro workers and have decided that their leaders are in the pay of employers to keep down organization. The union regards the organization of Negroes as "absolutely essential" to the success of all the workers, and would be willing to admit Negroes into their unions on the same terms, if they could get them. Several years ago during a strike, several truck companies brought in Negroes from the South to take their places. The strike was lost and in three large companies Negro workers continued. They work longer hours in order to earn the scale of the union teamsters, and have so resisted attempts at their organization that no other conclusion is possible but that they are being strongly influenced.

Negroes in the building trades face diverse conditions. As has been indicated there are only three Negro union carpenters in a total of 9,200 in three locals. The unions make no effort to enlist Negroes as members. Officials say that Negroes are "suspicious of not getting a square deal" and feel "dissatisfaction" with treatment in the organization. In one local there was complaint from white members when one Negro was taken in, but "gradually they came to accept him and have become friendly with him."

The bricklayers have met a more formidable situation. The white members are willing to take Negroes into the unions on equal terms and do not insist on separate locals. A Negro is vice-president of the local and another is a member of the important finance committee. The willingness to accept Negro bricklayers is due to the fact that there are many Negroes skilled in this work and "they can stir up trouble as strikebreakers and non-union men." It was because they were working independently at whatever wages they could get that they were taken into the bricklayer's local. Most of the Negroes are reported as being interested active members. They often complain of discrimination and it is true that certain foremen and contractors refuse to take Negro bricklayers. Usually the reason given is incompetence. Occasionally the boss says that the people he is working for will not have Negroes on the job. It is almost never that the foreman says that *he is* unwilling to work with Negroes. It is considered important to organize Negro labor "for the Negro's protection, and also to prevent his blocking the activities of the union", but if enough Negro members could be obtained, efforts would be made to have them form a separate local. Then there would be less friction.

For the rest, the general attitude of unions toward Negroes is in Los Angeles as it is almost everywhere throughout the country. Every union interviewed was strongly of the opinion that Negro organization was necessary for the aims of labor. This principle was not translated into practice, however, except where Negro labor was a menace as possible non-union workers or strikebreakers. The most generous relations have followed strikes when Negroes have secured the unions by coming into their midst. There is indifference and even hostility where employers bar Negroes in the first place. The whites do not like to associate with Negroes in large numbers and feel superior generally. Where employers object to Negroes or are indifferent to them, the unions are always ready to accept the situation without any feeling of responsibility for a change.*

DETROIT, MICHIGAN.

In a survey of Detroit it was difficult to get data on the Negro's standing in unions because of the attitude of the local federated labor body. The following table gives the number of Negro members as reported by several locals:

UNION	NUMBER OF NEGRO MEMBERS
Stewards (Great Lakes, etc.)	1,000
Laundry Workers (women)	300
Laborers	300
Bricklayers	200
Plasterers and Cement Mixers	100
Carpenters	73
Steel Car Men	45
Molders	30
Hoisting and Portable Engineers	10
Garment Workers	3
Typographical Union	2
Total	2,063

In the interracial commission's survey embracing 1,000 heads of Negro families, 34 reported union memberships, 843 reported that they were not members of a union, and 124 did not answer. The data secured by this study has an added interest because of the fact that reasons were given by Negroes for not belonging to a union:

Have no trade	175
No need to join	323
Too old, too much expense, or impossible	22
Do not join because of segregation	39
No answer	407

* Vide: Industrial Survey of the Negro Population of Los Angeles, California, National Urban League.

Some of the labor leaders interviewed look upon the Negro as a strikebreaker even though they frequently claim that he is such because he is the unconscious tool of a clever employer. Several labor leaders said that Negroes are taken in solely because they constitute a menace outside of the union. Many union officials were high in their praises of Negro members, saying they were as loyal as were the white members, sometimes more so.

Union officials were divided on what to do about the colored worker. The union which took him in admitted that it did not want him, in many cases. At other times it frankly stated that it could not give the Negro equal treatment, basing this discrimination on the employer's refusal to accept colored workmen. Other unions, while they barred the Negro by various devices, wanted him unionized in separate locals. Some officials expressed willingness to spend both time and money to help the colored men organize such locals. The unions which admit colored men object to this latter plan on the ground that it dissipates the strength of the union and also wastes a valuable opportunity for colored and white members to get together and thrash out their common problems, as well as their misunderstandings. In two joint unions with a membership of over 400, this mixed type of union had been found very successful and no trouble had arisen betwen colored and white members with employers. *

BUFFALO, N. Y.

Interest in labor organizations among Negroes is scarcely discernible. Buffalo is not a strong "union town" in spite of the large number of unions. There has always existed the conflict among white workers between common racial sentiment and the most abstract theorizations concerning collective bargaining. Both white and Negro workers agree in theory that the protection of all workers lies in organization, but in practice the white workers cannot bring themselves to accept the Negroes into equal opportunity with them for the same positions and pay, and the Negro workers have found that they are better able to get a job by bargaining direct with the employers. Thus matters stand. The leaders of the local unions are usually more liberal in the views and feeling about Negroes than members. The vice-president of the International Longshoremen's Union, located in Buffalo, represents the liberal type, but he admits that there are difficulties to organize any Negroes, both from the white members and from Negro indifference. There are relatively few

---

* Vide: The Negro in Detroit. The Mayor's Committee on International Cooperation.

Negro longshoremen organized although those who belong to unions make faultless members. During the strike at the dock an effort was made to organize the Negro longshoremen as a check upon their posible use to break the strike. This met with some little success. A few non-union workers struck out of sympathy with the strikers and in the end profited from pay increases. Scattered in several of the other trades groups may be found occasional Negro members, but since records are not kept by race and the number of Negroes is so small the actual extent of organization among Negroes could not be learned.

In 1927 there were 38 trade unions in Buffalo. Twelve unions excluded Negroes from membership. Dr. Carpenter points out in his study that unions "are quite frank in admitting that they can easily find some excuse to prevent the admission of Negro workmen." Local 12, of the Curb Setters and Asphalt Pavers operates under a closed shop agreement in Buffalo and refuses to admit Negroes. This is the sort of work generally done by Negroes in other cities. The tug firemen formally exclude the Negro worker principally because of the necessity of living and working with him in close quarters for long stretches. "The Cooks Union excludes Negro cooks, because it feels that the Negro is usually employed in a different kind of establishment from that employing union cooks, and because of a traditional policy of exclusion." [1]

ALBANY, N. Y.

The Albany Negro is largely distributed in the non-organized occupations, having no union jurisdiction. In the fields where there are Negro employees, the unions do not have Negro members. The unions of the printing trades, hotels and restaurant employees, building trades, journeymen barbers, report no Negro members. The Structural and Ornamental Iron Workers Union, No. 12, reported having one Negro member a few years ago. Since his death there have been no others. The hod carriers and building laborers union despite the member of Negroes employed in the trades, have no Negro members.

No special efforts have been made by any of the unions to secure Negro members, though some of the unions felt that all men should be admitted to the ranks of organized labor. One secretary states: "We should organize all Negroes that work

---

[1] Nationality, Color, and Economic Opportunity in the City of Buffalo, Niles Carpenter, University of Buffalo, 1927.

at any trade as they are just as essential to the labor movement as anyone else. I have noticed, however, that they are a little harder to handle than the white men. I mean they are a little harder to get to pay their dues and will go back to work quicker than the white men in places that they have had strikes. This may sound strange, but, I believe that if they were taken into the white man's confidence more this would not be so noticeable." *

TRENTON, N. J.

Organized labor in Trenton "suffers from a lack of a functioning central body". There are some 40 locals of different internationals in which Negroes have a very small representation excepting the hod carriers, which has 200 Negroes in a total of 250. This trade is practically 100 per cent organized. The folowing table indicates the total and Negro membership in the principal unions of Trenton:

NAME OF UNION	MEMBERSHIP TOTAL	MEMBERSHIP NEGRO
Barbers, Journeymen	107	—
Bricklayers, Masons and Plasterers	520	—
Carpenters	1,000	—
Decorators	150	—
Electricians	125	—
Freight Handlers and Station Employees	25	—
Garment Workers, United	250	—
Hod Carriers	250	200
Letter Carriers	89	7
Molders	50	—
Painters	300	2
Plumbers and Steamfitters	125	—
Potters, Operative	3,000	—
Sheet Metal Workers	75	—
Shop Crafts, Federated	1,900	—
Trolleymen's Unions	327	15
Turners and Handlers (Pottery)	60	—
Total		224

* Vide: A survey of the Negro Population of Albany, New York. National Urban League.

In the above table only four unions report Negro members. One, the hod carriers, has already been mentioned. All the Negro letter carriers are affiliated with their union and take a prominent part in its activities. Of the 15 Negroes in the trolleymen's union, 14 are power house employees, and one is a track greaser.

Except for the hod carriers and two painters, Negroes are not represented in the building trades unions. At one time four or five belonged to the bricklayers and a few were connected with the plumbers and steamfitters as helpers but in each case they dropped out. On the other hand, these unions have never made an effort to recruit Negro members.

In Trenton's great pottery industry a few Negroes who joined in times of labor shortage and strike still remain, but in the capacity of unskilled workers, and they are not in the unions, either the general union of pottery employees or those embracing the skilled operators. There exists a feeling of resentment toward those Negroes who acted as strikebreakers in 1922. One-third of all the members of the National Brotherhood of Operative Potters are located in Trenton.

There is every indication that the unions of Trenton in general are indifferent to Negro membership. Though union officials agree in saying that the organization of Negroes is essential to the labor movement they seem to accept the inevitability of hostility, discrimination and even exclusion of Negroes, those that are relieved of the necessity dealing with Negroes because there are none in the trade apparently considering themselves fortunate.[1]

SPRINGFIELD, ILLINOIS.

Mining is the chief industry in Springfield, and here is located a district headquarters of the United Mine Workers. Negroes are freely admitted to the union which they join just as freely. The unions in conjunction with the State provide a form of insurance against accident and death. The accident and mortality rate is exceedingly high.[2]

DENVER, COLORADO.

There are approximately 325 Negro members of unions in Denver. Of this number 125 belong to the Brotherhood of Sleep-

---

[1] Vide: A Survey of the Negro Population of Trenton, N. J. National Urban League.

[2] A Survey of the Negro Population of Springfield, Ill. National Urban League.

ing Car Porters and 115 to the Hod Carriers, Building and Common Laborers Union. The next largest group is a separate local of Negro musicians with 37 members. The National Association of Letter Carriers has as members all of the 23 Negroes employed in the post office. Eighteen Negro post office clerks are affiliated with the clerks union. An official of the carriers union says, "There have been a few small complications in a social way, but most of our men are intelligent and the social life is segregated. All business is on an equal footing." There are four Negroes in the bricklayers, 8 or 10 in the plasterers, and 10 in the city employees unions. The Journeymen Tailors union has one Negro member. For other Negro memberships there are no details. The following unions in Denver says they do not admit Negroes: printing pressmen, painters, electrical workers, railway mail association, plumbers and gasfitters. The musicians direct Negroes to the Negro local already mentioned. The waiters and waitresses union claims to accept Negroes, but only to form a separate local. Such an organization was once formed but soon failed because "Negroes don't see the need of organization," and "cease to function in a short time." The Mailers union has "no law against Negro members, but there are few in the trade." The United Slate, Tile and Composition Roofers union does not have any Negro members, but believes that all workers should be organized. The secretary of the Bricklayers union (previously mentioned), reported good relationships with Negro members, despite the fact that Negroes "as a rule are not proficient."

An example of how the employment of Negroes may affect the relationship of a plant with organized labor, the following case is cited. A Negro who for eighteen years has been an employee of a firm making inks and rollers necessary to printing in places where the altitude will not permit the use of ordinary equipment. Five years ago he was made superintendent of the roller-making department. Despite his evident efficiency, the Roller Makers union having jurisdiction over the processes, will neither grant him membership, nor his two under-employees who also are Negroes. [1]

Worcester, Mass.

Replies were received from but two labor unions, Local No. 186, Journeymen Barbers International Union of America, and

---

[1] Vide: The Social and Economic Status of the Negro Population of Denver, Colorado. National Urban League, 1929.

the Worcester Musicians Association, Local No. 143, A. F. of M. Both of these unions say they admit Negroes to full membership. The former has two Negro members and the latter three at the present time. The total membership is 156 and 548 respectively.

There have been no strikes in the past history of these locals where the question of the relations of the white and Negro workers have come up.

The Barbers Union says that it has made an effort to get Negro members but without much success. Negroes give their inability to get work in the white shops as their reason for not joining the union. They did not see how membership in the union will aid them. Those who belong are admitted on exactly the same terms as applied to the white candidates. But relationship between the white and colored members were reported as "pleasant" and the organization of the colored barbers is regarded by the union officials as essential to the success of the labor movement.

The Musicians local expressed the belief that "in order to be a success a labor organization should never recognize class, creed or color." Its methods of getting Negro members have been the same as those used to get whites in and they claim to have met with "fair" success. Negroes are admitted on an equal basis and relations are friendly.

The officials reported that the Negro members tend to drop out. The reason given is usually the non-payment of dues.[1]

YOUNGSTOWN, OHIO

The secretary of the Central Labor Union in Youngstown estimates that 90 per cent of the organized workers of the city are in the building trades, including bricklayers, carpenters, lathers, composition roofers, cement finishers, plasterers, building laborers, painters, electricians. This probably underestimates the numerical but not the economic importance of the other trade unions, streetcar men, barbers, musicians, mail carriers, garment workers, printers, stationary engineers, etc. With the exception of one small local of the Amalgamated Steel, Iron and Tin Workers, the steel mill workers, by far the largest number of Youngstown's wage-earners, are entirely unorganized. It is estimated that there may be a thousand railroad workers in Youngstown who belong to vari-

---

[1] Vide: The Negro Population of Worcester, Mass. National Urban League, 1929.

ous trade unions, but they are usually members of locals at railroad terminals rather than where they live.

No one knew of any unfairness in the present attitude of any of the building trades unions toward Negro workers. It was pointed out by both white union officials and by keen colored observers that the scarcity of skilled building trades workers,—evidenced by an actual wage scale considerably higher than the union scale,—removes all fear of the Negro as a competitor so long as he is within the union. The business agents of the Painters and Electricians Unions, which have no colored workers, insisted that properly qualified applicants would be admitted regardless of color. A Negro electrician said that though there were no Negroes in the union he did not know of any rule against them.

There are three colored members in the carpenters' union, and a colored contractor who employs both colored and white union carpteners asserted that he had never known of any trouble between them. A colored social worker, J. ——, who is a carpenter by trade, however, told of his experience with this union when he came to Youngstown twelve years ago to prove that the attitude has not always been cordial. Upon the advice of friends he joined the union immediately. Although there were very few Negroes in the city at that time, three of them belonged to the carpenters union. They, however, usually found their own jobs and worked by themselves with little intercourse with their white fellow unionists. On the night of his initiation, J—— overheard the secretary whisper to the president,—"Do I have to find a job for J—— too?" In spite of the president's nod, J—— walked the streets for thirty days looking for work and receiving no help whatever from the union.

There were five colored men among the charter members in the bricklayers' union when it was organized in 1886. For twenty years one colored man was a member of the board of trustees, one of the most honored positions in the gift of this union. Another was president, and others have served on the executive committee and on numerous adjustment committees. A white official of this union asserted vigorously, "Three of our colored members are as intelligent as any people in Youngstown, barring none!" Apparently relations between the men of the two races in this union are better than in any other group, union or otherwise, in the city.

Most of the *cement finishers,* most of the *composition roofers,* and most of the *building laborers* are Negroes. These unions are all receiving the support of the other more powerful building trades unions. Although organized several years ago, the union of building laborers has only recently demanded recognition and full union status. During the past summer three strikes have been called by all the building trades unions to force such recognition. Just now operations are proceeding under a truce whereby members of the laborers unions are not discriminated against but full recognition is not to be insisted upon until May 1, when wage agreements for all the building trades including the laborers will be made. White union officials believe that the difficulty in securing recognition for the building laborers' union lies not in the fear of demands for excessive wages, since wages now being paid are higher than any probable union demand, nor in objection to union organizations, since all the other building trades have won union rcognition, rather in the unwillingness of white contractors to negotiate with Negro laborers.

Outside the building trades the unions do not play an important role in Youngstown, and the Negroes do not play an important role in the unions. Nevertheless, the experiences and attitudes of some Negroes in these other occupations seem significant.

The Musicians union in Youngstown as in most cities has two locals,—one with more than 1,000 white members and the other with 20 or 30 colored members. Membership in either local entitled one to attendance at meetings of both. Colored members have sometimes availed themselves of the privilege of attending meetings of the white local and have always been courteously treated, usually being asked to make a speech. White members, however, have not returned their visits. The colored men want a separate local because it enables them to negotiate a lower scale of prices with their colored patrons whose average economic resources are less than the resources of the white patrons. The agreement between the two locals provides that white patrons must pay the scale of prices set by the white local whether they employ white or colored musicians, and that colored patrons must pay the same scale to white musicians, but a lower scale to colored musicians. Neither of the musicians' locals is affiliated to the central labor body. After careful consideration the colored local decided against affiliation for two reasons,—first, the expense disproportionate to the advantages to so small a local of this kind; and second, the fear of "embarrassment" from failure to receive a due share of the patronage of the other unions upon which they would feel obliged to insist if they were affiliated.

The president of the musicians' union is also a mail carrier and like all the other mail carriers in Youngstown a member of the mail carriers' association. Twelve of the 100 mail carriers are colored. Colored men have been members of this union since its inception but have never been elected to any office except that once a colored man was elected as delegate to the national convention. One reason for the lack of interest of colored members lies in the dances and card parties financed from the association's treasury, while the tacit agreement between the races forbids the colored members to attend even if they wanted to.

Southern Cities

The American Federation of Labor is now perfecting plans for organizing the southern workers. Though the initial effort is to be centered on the organization of textile workers, the problem of Negro workers cannot be ignored either in the organized or unorganized industries. However before any success can be achieved in their organization, the trade unions of the South must clean house. Some officials of the Federation are of the opinion that the present methods of organizing Negro workers is successful, and that the problems involved as they affect the relationship of Negro workers are overestimated. According to Charles H. Franck, Organizer of the American Federation of Labor:

"The Negro problem assumes a place wholly out of proportion to its real position. Organized labor in the South can and will solve the problem to the good and welfare of all concerned and the membership is learning to pay little if any attention to the suggestion coming from those not connected with the labor movement; but also too often are insistent that "this or that should be done." Profiting by past experience the union membership in the South will find in the not distant future the solution of this question and it will not be by cussing the nigger" and engaging in a cut-throat competition for opportunities for earning a living. This being an economic question the solution will be found as other problems have been solved—by treating it as an economic question."[1]

It happens however that organized labor in many instances does not treat the matter as an "economic question." To wit:

1—The twenty-ninth annual convention of the Mississippi Association of Rural Letter Carriers in July, 1929. "Ef-

---

[1] Southern Labor—The American Federationist, pp. 1460-1461. Dec. 1928. Vol. 35, No. 12.

forts to change the constitution so as to strike out the section limiting membership to white carriers opened a heated argument which was stopped when President Mc-Fadden suggested that the constitution in that regard remain without amendment." [1]

2—Because the proposed plan of the City Manager of New Orleans, Louisiana, provides for a civil service "that places the Negro on the same basis with the whites and will not prevent his exclusion, the Central Trades and Labor Council, white has voted against the measure." [2]

3—"The labor fakers of the Brotherhood of Railway Firemen have signed a new agreement with the Atlantic Coast Line Road, which in its race discrimination features again shows the Negro workers that reactionary American Labor has nothing to do with them. Under the new contract at least 51 per cent of the firemen on the Atlantic Coast Line must be white. It is understood that the railroad has agreed not to employ Negro firemen and in the future new vacancies will be filled with white firemen." [3]

4—"It has been hinted that the American Federation of Labor will initiate a diplomatic policy in its Southern campaign. It will be a back-to-the-farm movement for the Negro. With industry coming South, requiring large bodies of labor and paying better wages than tenant farming in most instances, although the farm needs are pressing, the union organization can see a benefit in shifting Negroes onto the farm and the whites into the factory." [4]

5—The Barbers Protective Association of Virginia, composed of colored journeymen barbers, in opposing the Virginia barbers licensing bill is fighting a real and not an imaginary threat to their trade and economic existence. This bill is sponsored by the Journeymen Barbers Association, a white organization, and having the backing of the Master

Barbers Association of America and the American Federation of Labor, passed the Senate of the 1928 General Assembly but failed of a majority vote in the House. It is certain to be re-introduced in the 1930 Legislature.[5]

---

[1] Memphis (Tenn) Commercial Appeal, July 21, 1929.
[2] Associated Negro Press Dispatch, June 26, 1929.
[3] Red Bank (N. J.) Echo, December 15, 1929.
[4] St. Louis (Mo.) Argres November 29, 1929.
[5] The Norfolk (Va.) Journal and Guide, August 3, 1929.

6—"At the edge of many of the Southern mill villages is 'nigger town,' a short stretch of road flanked by small, unpainted cottages which have the general appearance of being run down at the heels. Its houses are usually without lights and running water, and in many cases they are owned by private realtors. The few Negro workers of the mills may trade at the same stores with white workers, but every other part of their social life is distinct. They are a minority rigidly confined to a few rooms in the mill and a few houses outside of the mill village.

"In practice the Negro men are employed only on the heaviest and most dirty manual labor while the women do the cleaning. The men unload the cotton from trucks, unwrap the bales and start the cotton through the cleaning process. When the cloth is completed, they sometimes pack it and load it for shipment. In one or two mills of the South they work at the least complicated machine processes, but that is only in case there are enough Negroes for a full room. They average less than 10 per cent of the workers of the mill, and in North Carolina they average less than 5 per cent." Their pay is uniformly below that of the white workers.

"The feeling of the white workers against any further employment of Negroes in the mills is intense. Two or three times in the history of cotton mill labor struggles the white workers have become inflamed with rumors concerning the use of Negro strikebreakers. Attacks upon the Negro population have followed. In the Macon strike of 1919 2 Negro women workers were killed and several wounded. No mill owner or superintendent would dare to employ Negroes for the regular work now done by whites unless they attempted to operate a mill exclusively by Negro labor. The rule against Negroes and whites working in the same room has the sanctity of a law. In 1921, a mill superintendent of South Carolina was fined $110 'for working employees over 60 hours a week and for allowing members of both races to work in the same room.'

"The South does not seem to have made a fair test yet of the Negroes' capacity for factory adaptation. The experiments already undertaken have labored under special difficulties. The Negroes may yet prove their ability to operate exclusively Negro mills, but their entrance into the cotton mills at the present time as a major group would be a most uphappy event for the white workers. The wages and living standards of the white workers would be even further undermined. Racial conflict of the most bitter sort would inevitably follow, since the feeling of hostility between the "poor whites" and Negroes is traditional."[1]

7—"There are two central bodies here in New Orleans: The Central Trades and Labor Council, white, and the Central Labor Union for the colored workers. This in itself is a duplication of effort and creates an artificial division in the labor movement. Some of the unions who admit colored toilers to their membership are affiliated with both central bodies, and this is the irony of the situation; the Central Trades and Labor Council is restricted to white people, while the Central Labor Union is open to all, white or colored."[2]

Concrete examples of similar shortcomings could be continued, for, despite the fact that a few organized workers in the south realize the necessity for labor organizations existing above racial lines, the rank and file, and in many cases the leaders, are in no sense ready to remove the remaining vestiges of the slave regime. The actual situation is best portrayed through the following summaries of investigations in selected southern cities.

JACKSONVILLE, FLORIDA

Negroes are losing traditional jobs because white workers are getting first call on them. Hence a northward migration continues. In February, 1928, the city council voted down an ordinance presented by certain labor interests wherein Negro workers would be confined to the construction and repairing of buildings and residences in city blocks occupied exclusively by Negroes. More recently, however, the council passed a taxicab law making it unlawful for Negro cabmen to haul white passengers and white cabmen to haul Negro passengers.

Labor unions have a relatively low status, many of them having lost more than half of their memberships because of increased open shop activity. Colored and white workers have separate unions, which have little or no connections with each other—

---

[1] Blanshard, Paul. Labor in Southern Cotton Mills, p. 67.
[2] Schad. Herman J.—American Federationist, Vol. 35, No. 11. November 1928. p. 1364.

neither group seems to have any interest in the other. There are approximately 200 organized colored workers in Jacksonville.

ATLANTA, GEORGIA

Though the Secretary of the Atlanta Trades and Labor Council admitted the prejudices of union workers against Negroes, he cited instances where white and colored mechanics are working harmoniously on buildings being constructed in that city. The greatest damage done to organized labor in the building trades, according to Mr. Lynch, was done by Negro carpenters who are, as are the white carpenters, poorly organized. Employers' and manufacturers' organizations in Atlanta are hostile to trades unions but the public is said to have a favorable attitude. There are approximately 300 organized Negro workers in Atlanta.

BIRMINGHAM, ALABAMA

At the seat of the A. F. of L.'s southern campaign Negro workers have lost numerous industrial positions. The Tennessee Coal & Iron Company, however, employs Negro workers, skilled, semiskilled, and unskilled in large numbers.

Because white union brickmasons will not work on jobs with Negro masons, the latter group is limited in its employment despite membership in the brickmasons union. There were 255 organized Negro workers in Birmingham in May, 1928. (Excluding independent Negro unions.) The status of the unions is fair, they being strong enough to maintain union wages and conditions. A large number of workers, particularly colored ones, work for non-union wages. The United Mine Workers union has gone to pieces there being only one local in the state with 11 members, located at Lehigh, Alabama. The secretary of the Alabama State Federation of Labor reported in December, 1929, that 75 per cent of the organizable Negro workers in Alabama were unorganized, that miners were earning $4.25 a day and averaging three days a week, and that common laborers received from $2.00 to $4.50 a day.

CHARLESTON, S. C.

This city had at one time the most highly organized group of Negro workers in the country. In 1928 the industrial employment of Negroes had reached such an acute state that Negro building mechanics, contractors, business and professional men had assembled to discuss methods by which this situation could be remedied.

Negro workers were losing their grip on the building trades. More and more white workers were objecting to working with Negroes. Union men, particularly carpenters, had walked off jobs when Negroes were employed. In 1928 there were approximately 500 organized building tradesmen in 3 locals. The carpenters had about 200 members, though the number had been as high as 700 some years previous. The Bricklayers Union had 68 members only 8 of whom were white.

Negro workers though belonging to the unions have been forced to work at a lower scale than white union workers in order to secure employment. White workers, apparently, have condoned this method. In 1925 and 1926 a publicity program instituted by the Charleston Board of Trade is said to have resulted in the importation of white mechanics. Shortly thereafter when a white contractor refused to hire Negro workers on the construction of a Negro school this fact became public. As a result the Directors of the Board of Trade resigned. Later the organization was revived and is still active and effective in some circles.*

During the World War the freighthandlers of the Atlantic Coast Line organized a local labor union. This body is now inactive, because of the great turnover in employment, and the general weakness of its bargaining ability.

White men are teamsters today. Negroes formerly performed this service to the exclusion of all other workmen. Streets are cleaned by white men, while asphalt paving is done by Negroes. Longshoremen are Negroes and 400 of them are organized in a local of that union. Today white men are scavengers in Negro districts. Three years ago Negroes laughted when white men were seen digging streets for sewer pipes. Today it is the exception to see colored men employed.

Some responsibility for losses in occupations is attributed to the weaknesses of Negro workers. One company employed approximately 300 Negroes in its plant. When the company was forced to stop operations on a certain day because so many of the Negro workers "lay off" to go to a picnic, its employment policy was revised. Since that time Negro workers have been replaced by whites as vacancies occurred.

* Report of T. Arnold Hill, Director of Industrial Relations, National Urban League, 1928.

NASHVILLE, TENNESSEE

The Negro workers of Nashville are employed in a wide range of occupations. In railway shops, machine shops and mills generally. Negroes are employed mostly as helpers. There are a few Negro brickmasons who are sometimes employed on jobs with white workmen but more often on separate jobs. Negro contractors employ a large number of Negro workers in the building trades. According to labor officials 350 Negroes are members of trades unions in the city.

PENSACOLA, FLORIDA

Of the 1,500 organized workers in Pensacola, 350 are said to be Negroes. There is an attempt to displace Negroes in certain lines of employment, especially in the building trades. Because of the scarcity of employment in 1928 efforts were exerted on contractors to induce them to hire all white workers on building projects. As a case in point, a city official attempted to force the contractor on a municipal project to use all white employees. The contract was withheld for one week because the contractor refused to agree to the suggestion, stating that there were a number of Negro workers who would be used, and if any whites applied for work they would be given employment just as Negroes would he hired.*

AIKEN, S. C.

Aiken has no Central Labor Union, and the investigator could find no local of white workers. Such white workers as were organized held union cards in locals outside of Aiken. There was one colored local union, the Bricklayers and Plasterers Union No. 14. These men do most of the brickmasonry in the city. Locals of carpenters and painters existing sometime ago are no longer active.

COLUMBUS, GEORGIA

It is estimated that there are 70 organized Negro workers in Columbus. Less than ten years ago there were six colored locals in the city. All of these have now gone to pieces.

MOBILE, ALABAMA

Negro workers do the major portion of street paving and of common labor in the lumber industry in Mobile. A high percentage of firemen on the Louisville and Nashville Railroad in this

---

* Dabney, Thomas L.—Field Investigation.

district is Negroes. About 3,000 Negroes are said to be employed on the Mobile waterfront.

Union membership among Negroes is estimated at 650. Some unions, as longshoremen's locals—white and colored—have weakened considerably during the last five years as have the building trades groups. White and Negro workers are drifting apart and much prejudice is said to exist among whites against the Negroes. The president of the Central Trades Council of Mobile, Alabama, states that:

"The situation in Mobile with reference to Negro membership in Labor organizations is similar to that in many other cities. The local unions follows procedure of other local unions elsewhere. The carpenters have encouraged the organization of Negro carpenters and there is a separate local union holding a charter from the United Brotherhood. The bricklayers, plasterers and lathers have mixed local unions and function well together. The longshoremen have separate local unions. The sentiment on the part of the other trades is not near as strong against the Negroes as it was some three years ago for the average white man has seen that the Negro is an economic factor and a competitor.

"The Central Trades Council has been advocating and encouraging the organization of the Negro workers. At one time or another we have some opposition on the part of a good "100" percenter, but this has not deterred the work and we hope and expect to go down the line and having everything organized that works for a living.

"The Negro in Mobile is largely led by men who are exploiters. On a number of occasions they have had good organizations only to have them wrecked by some one of their own color working as an agent for some outside interest.

"In recent months the longshoremen had a struggle. The employers succeeded in getting many of the Negroes to drop out. They organized a "rump" Union. Wages of course dropped to nothing. The white man came off the ships and is now devoting his efforts towards making a living by loading only Shipping Board ships. The Negroes, working for the white stevedores, wanted more money several weeks ago. A meeting was called and addressed by the chairman of the employers who soon convinced the Negroes that the wages could not be raised and so they went back to work at wages less than before.

"When the white man in the South who works for a living finally wakes up to the fact that the opposition towards organizing the Negroes comes from the same source which is opposed to organization generally, he will do what the bricklayers and plasterers have done to their good, namely organize the workers irrespective of any foolishness of white man's supremacy.

"The hesitancy on the part of many Negroes to join a Union is the fact that previous organizations have been wrecked by men of their own color and the lack of cooperation from the white man. It is my firm belief that if the Negro was assured of support and assistance (moral) he would be 100 per cent for organized labor.

"Another thing is the failure on the part of the Negro preachers and ministers to encourage the Negro wage-earner. This element I sometimes believe secures financial aid for their churches on the promise to discourage their own race from becoming members of legitimate labor unions.

"The Central Trades Council here is now endeavoring again to have the Negro union members represented in a Negro central council of their own, securing a charter from the American Federation of Labor. I believe that, for the time being this would enable a more thorough discussion of the subject both white and Negro are interested in. My observation is that in a mixed central council or even a mixed assembly of any sort and kind, while there are men of the Negro race who have good constructive thoughts and ideas they feel hesitancy in securing the floor. For a short time I am contending then the organizing of the Negroes into a council of their own, committees from both to exchange visits each meeting night and a joint Executive Board."

RICHMOND, VIRGINIA

Labor unions in Richmond are confined largely to railway workers, bricklayers, plasterers and letter carriers. Negro bricklayers and plasterers, practicaularly the former, have lost their monopoly of these occupations. Practically no attempt has been made to effect any working relations between the two racial groups. Contractors will not work white and colored bricklayers on the same job. Five thousand Negro tobacco workers are unorganized. The survey of Negroes in Richmond pointed out that it "was unable to secure any information from the local headquarters about the number of Negro men or women who belong to trade union organizations. [1]

NORFOLK, VIRGINIA

Thirteen hundred Negro workers in Norfolk are said to be organized. The labor union status among longshoremen, railway workers, and garment workers is high. Except for the longshoremen the unskilled workers white and colored are unorganized.

CHATTANOOGA, TENNESSEE

There is no cooperation between organized Negro and white labor in Chattanooga except through the individual efforts of one or two of the most intelligent and energetic white and colored men. The early experiences of the molders in attempting to organize Negro workers in this city has undoubtedly left its imprint for no more than 175 workers were found organized. On the other hand there are approximately 135 Negro boiler workers in the city.

LOUISVILLE, KENTUCKY

Except for the fact that contractors will not employ white and Negro brickmasons, plasters or carpenters on the same jobs, relations betwen white and Negro labor in Louisville are said to be normal. In the city there are large Negro groups of boilermakers, molders and tobacco workers, mainly unorganized. The 474 organized Negro workers are chiefly bricklayers and the carpenters have mixed unions, though the colored members seldom attend meetings. The hod carriers union is 95 per cent colored.

KNOXVILLE, TENNESSEE

The local of Negro freighthandlers in this city failed, partly because the rest of the colored freight handlers on the Southern Railroad System were not organized, making recognition of the union impossible, and partly because of the establishment of a dual organization of freighthandlers.

No Southern A. F. of L. official has been more outspoken in his denunciation of organized labor's practice in the matter of Negro workers than President Schad, of the New Orleans Bakers" Union No. 35. In New Orleans there are two or three labor unions composed entirely of colored workers who have their trades completely organized and enjoy favorable working conditions.

---

[1] The Negro in Richmond, Virginia; the report of the Negro Welfare Survey Committee, 1929. p. 19.

Some unions in the city, however, bar Negro workers entirely, and will not take them under any circumstances. Local No. 35 of the bakers since its inception in 1885 had restricted its membership to whites but in 1918 because there were more than 100 colored bakers working at the trade the restriction was removed. Today there a number of colored workers in the union. Then a problem arises—the union cannot force employers to hire Negro bakers. What price organization for these workers?

All trades have undoubtedly experienced the irony of the Negro workers situation as expressed by the bakers union.

"Colored bakers do very well as long as they are organized and can be had cheaply and are not too particular as to hours and conditions; but the minute a shop becomes organized the colored bakers immediately become incompetent and undesirable, and they are then excluded from that shop until some opportune time, such as a strike or lockout, when they are again welcome.[1]

The most important phase underlying the organization of Negro workers in the South is the belief that (1) Negro workers in the South are unorganizable, (2) that their organization is undesirable. According to a university professor, modern industrialism is fast destroying the "old type of Southern darkey."[2] Furthermore, if it is true that Negroes cannot be induced to form a strong labor organization because of their unstable character. Then "there is less hope than ever that unionism will become strong among Southern Negroes, for the newer type is far less dependable, far less stable in character, than the former type." But, "let any group of Negroes form themselves into a labor organization, and they will find in most communities not only that their jobs are filled by other Negroes, but that as union members they are undesirables whose presence will not be tolerated in that community."

On the one hand is the half-hearted interest, and sometimes the total lack of interest of labor leaders who either organize Negroes in separate locals that have little or no bargaining power, often competing with white locals, or do not organize Negroes under any circumstances. On the other hand is the reactionary and paternalistic community anxious to maintain a docile and contented working class, be it white or colored, but who, if forced to accept organized labor will accept that labor on condition it is

[1] Schad. Herman J.—Organizing the Bakers, The American Federationist, Vol. 35, No. 11. November, 1928.
[2] Bonnett. Clarence T.—The Industrialization of the South in Relation to Labor. American Federationist, Vol. 35, No. 11. p. 1309.

white, or not at all,—unless the Negro is in the postion to put such a premium on his services, that he must be employed. Between these two groups are (1) the small band of Negro workers who are organized, or are willing to be organized—struggling for existence and (2) the unorganized Negro workers both skilled and unskilled, unlettered in the tenets of collective bargaining and who see their only hope in accepting employment as it is found, and under conditions that, unsatisfactory as they are, definitely assure them of a job and an income.

STRIKES AND NEGRO WORKERS

Shadowing the whole issue is the clouded social, economic and racial structure of the South wherein the Negro worker occupies a caste lower than the whites in all things economic and social, a structure which many labor organizations themselves perpetuate. Until organized labor is willing and ready to construct in policy and practice an organization scheme of the South the Negro worker will continue to doubt the efficacy of his affiliation.

Strikebreaking has been one method by which thousands of Negro workers have entered industries not previously employing them. In the majority of cases the provocateurs of Negro strikebreakers have been the employers and their representatives rather than the Negro himself. The inducements of higher wages, shorter hours and better work conditions than he previously enjoyed were more powerful arguments that the immorality of preventing the rise of the laboring groups then on strike. In fact, the strike in America involves the question of races as well as class. Negroes are not merely workers; they are black workers. Furthermore they are unorganized and threaten the economic security of the organized group. They are the most individualistic of workers and as yet have no body of sentiment to guide their group decisions and movements either toward the established labor organizations or the protection of employers. Each Negro worker is by most obvious circumstances encouraged to seek his immediate advantage.

The position of the Negro worker makes him important in any strike crisis, and his position is most hazardous. He may be used to further the ends both of anti-union employers and the unions. Whatever the difference between capital and white labor they seem agreed on one thing: that Negro workers are not entitled to the same privileges as white workers. If a strike is on, or threatens, the employers bid for their services with arguments having the impelling persuasion of a job when "one's family is hungry". The ending of a strike often means that the Negro is again out of a job. Unions consequently moralize but not until the Negro worker has been vigorously stigmatized as a strikebreaker and fermenter of race riots.

At the time of the 1919 steel strike the National Committee for organizing Iron and Steel Workers indicated that the Steel industry recruited and shipped from 30,000 to 40,000 Negroes into the mills as strikebreakers.[1] Many of them were picked up in northern cities, but the majority came from the South. These Negroes were a big factor in breaking the strike. In the Homestead works 1,737 of the 14,687 workers were Negroes—between 12 and 14 per cent. During the organizing campaign only eight joined the union. In Duquesne, Pa., where 344 Negroes were employed none struck; in Clairton, Pa., 6 per cent. of the 300 Negro workers joined the unions and struck for two weeks. Of the several hundred workers in the Braddock, Pa., plants, not one joined a union or went on strike; "and a dozen would cover those from the larger mills in Pittsburgh proper who walked out with the 25,000 whites. Similar tendencies were shown in the Chicago, Buffalo, Pueblo, Youngstown and Sparrows Point (Md.) districts. "In the entire steel industry, the Negroes, beyond compare, gave the movement less cooperation than any other element, skilled or unskilled, foreign or native."[2]

In the railroad strike of 1922 Negro workers were used in large number to take the places of the striking men that the operation of railroads might continue. Hundreds of Negro workers went into the shops as strikebreakers, while a number almost as large remained out and respected the grievances of their fellow workers. This, despite the fact that practices and policies of the transportation unions in excluding Negro workers have been most questionable, if not capricious.

The strike in the Chicago packing houses in 1917-1918 was waged when many men had been hopelessly idle for many months. The employment offices at the Yards were opened and deluged with applicants, white and colored. Because they formed 14,000 of the 65,000 workers in the industry, the Negroes became a strong factor. The unions were determined to organize them, and induced them to join a miscellaneous local with the understanding that later they would be transferred to the local unions

---

[1] Foster, Wm. Z. The Great Steel Strike, p. 207.
[2] Ibid.

of their individual crafts. When many of these crafts refused to accept them, the Negroes remained grouped in the Amalgamated Meat Cutters and Butchers Union. This circumstances did not strengthen the loyalty even of the Negro union men, to say nothing of the non-union worker and the unemployed prospective strikebreakers. Furthermore, not all the Negro or white union members struck, since many had voted for the shop representation plan, which was said to be at the root of the trouble.

Another version of the situation is given by Foster [1] who maintains that the Negro intellectual frustrated all organizing efforts.

No sooner had organizers begun the work than they met the firm opposition of the Negro intelligensia. These warned their people to have nothing to do with the movement, as their interest lay in working with the packers to defeat the unions. They said that was how the Negroes came into the packing industry, and that was how they would progress in it.

To such propaganda the organizers replied by launching a vigorous campaign to enlist Negroes.

Then the propaganda was sent forth that the only reason the whites were willing to take the blacks into their locals was because the latter, being in a minority, could exert no control; that the whites would not dare to give them a local of their own.

When a separate local for Negroes was established the "Jim Crow" cry was raised, which the organizers answered by insisting upon a free transfer system between the white and Negro locals —and "although the unions kept a crew of Negro organizers in the field and won many concessions for the workers, including the eight hour day, right of colective bargaining, wage increases, forty-hour week guarantee, seniority rights, etc." they never completely organized the Negroes—*nor the whites*. (Italics ours.)

As a result of this strike Negro workers in packing houses secured one of their first opportunities for occupational advancement. Electricians, steamfitters and carpenters were introduced for the first time in two of the large companies.

In the union of the mining industry Negroes have played the dual role of strikers and strikebreakers to a greater extent than in any other organization. As a result of their importation as

---

[1] Op. Cit.

strikebreakers towns composed entirely of Negroes have been formed. Because of their striking they have shown their respect for the principles of collective bargaining. In the Western Pennsylvania and West Virginia strike of 1927, Negro workers were imported in large numbers from southern fields. A smaller number came frm the West Virginia and Ohio fields. At the same time ther were a number of Negroes who were members of the union, and who struck with the white miners.

The fact that Negroes are members of unions does not mean that Negro strikebreakers' will not be employed. Within the past five years notable instances of such situations have been noted in strikes of that date and fig workers in Chicago, the paper box makers, furriers, garment workers, and laundry workers in New York, and the longshoremen.

In New York when the longshoremen on Piers 4, 18 and 19, North River and Pier 15 on East River struck for higher wages more than 500 Negro workers were rushed in to work on piers where colored longshoremen were not usualy hired. The strikers —chiefly Irish—had been receiving 75 cents an hour for eight hours and 85 cents an hour for overtime. They were demanding $1.00 an hour for straight time and $2.00 for overtime. The Negro strikebreakers were paid 85 cents for straight time and $1.00 for overtime. A compromise between workers and employers stopped the strike, though Negro workers were not retained on these piers.

During August 1929 the white longshoremen of Boston struck, when asked to double their loads. 125 Negroes were hired to replace the strikers. Because no Negroes ever had a "real chance" to work on the Boston docks, this was regarded as an opportunity to secure such employment as well as union protection.

Strikes in which Negro workers are involved have provoked violent racial clashes. The *white man's job* is being given to Negroes. The situation in its whole cloth has been summed up as a lamentable fact:

"That there is a large and influential black leadership— who as a matter of race tactics are violently opposed to their people going into the trade unions. They look upon strikebreaking as a legitimate and effective means of Negro advancement. They have seen their people, by use of it, readily work their way into trades and industries previously firmly sealed against them by the white workers and white employers prejudices." [1]

On the other hand the most practical approach that has been made by Negroes who have advised workers on strikes and strike-breaking is a strike in an industry, the union by in no way countenancing strikebreaking against those unions that have been fair and equal in the admission of Negro workers, and subsequently fair and equal in their treatment of Negro workers after they became members of that union.

Six hundred local organizations replied to the question on strike experience with Negro workers. In 263 of these locals Negroes had participated in strikes in one of the following forms. One hundred and thirty-nine of the 263 locals either refused membership to Negroes or had none as members.

NEGROES INVOLVED IN STRIKES AS:	NUMBER OF LOCALS
Fellow Unionists	122
Strikebreakers	71
Non-union Men Working in Plants	27
Fellow Unionists and Strikebreakers	43

EXPERIENCES OF NEGRO WORKERS WITH UNIONS

1—D. W. has been a construction laborer and coal hiker ever since coming to ——, nine years ago. He joined a local of the teamsters union and received the regular union scale—$4.00 a day. He finds no fault with unions but does wish that agents would properly record the payments of dues and give receipts when they are paid.

2—R. W. belongs to the same local and came from Montgomery, Ala., in 1921, where he had been employed as a painter. He had no trouble in joining the union. Since being a member he has earned from $4.00 to $6.00 daily as a coal hiker, but the union does not enforce its work agreements.

3—J. A. has been a union man for fifteen years. Trained as a plumber he experienced too great a difficulty in securing ade-

---
[1]Foster, p. 210.

quate work in that field. He then became a well digger and now earns $9.60 per day. He has worked regularly, and has received all of the union benefits, including sick benefits.

4—A. H. is a carpenter and a member of the carpenters union in C—. The $1.37½ wage per hour is quite attractive, but he has found it impossible to get enough work to keep busy, as the union gives no aid in securing work for Negroes.

5—J. C. is a molder by trade though now employed as a filling station attendant. Finding it difficult to secure permanent employment at his trade he took his present job at $145.00 a month. He has found no trouble in maintaining desirable union affiliations and has found his membership profitable because of regular employment and higher wages.

6—R. P. M. is a union bricklayer and plasterer in a northern city who has been kept busy, has received standard wages and feels "lost" without the union.

7—P. S. is a union laborer who believes that there is some advantage in belonging to the unions but not as they are now managed. Despite his membership he is forced to work at a scale lower than that set by the Union. In barbering the "union card amounts to nothing except where the shop is patronized by entirely white trade or nearly so."

8—As a musician C. H. has found membership in the Musician's Protective Association extremely profitable. When working he earns $72.00 per week.

9—T. P. admits that he was literally forced to join the Cleaners and Dyers Union of which he is a member. It was not until the 1919 strike in —— that Negroes were able to get jobs in pressing and tailoring shops. Now that Negroes are members of unions they get higher pay. On the other hand one gets the cleaning done easier and the service is better. Yet, cleaning establishments will not collect your clothes unless you are in the union. When asked in what way unions can prove harmful the terse reply was "pineapples."

10—J. J. has been a union laborer for seven years. He has found the wages of $7.00 a day when working very attractive. Membership has also meant obtaining more work.

11—J. H., a cement finisher and plasterer by trade, but on coming to C—, was forced to take work as a laborer. When plying his trade in P—, he was a member of the local union for five years. On the basis of that experience he maintains that such gain as is forthcoming in higher wages when working, is lost because of discrimination in assignment of work when it is normal. There is "to much discrimination."

12—H. H. has been a carpenter for twenty years, and a member of the carpenters union for fifteen years. He has received the same consideration as other workers. A few times since the war workmen have walked off the job because he was employed but he was always retained.

13—I. B. has been a lather for seventeen years. Once he belonged to the lathers union, but found no value in it for colored workers unless there was an unusual amount of building. "The white men were sent out on the jobs and colored are not given work. It is better to work independently."

14— —— is a longshoreman who now belongs to a company union, but only because the local to which he belonged lost a strike some years ago. Organized labor, he believes, "is the salvation of the working man, white or black."

15—D. B. is an expert bricklayer and always employed. He is a member of the union of his craft and "believes in unions absolutely."

16—H. B. L. has been a barber for forty-one years. By belonging to the barbers union he has benefited through shorter hours and better pay.

17—W. K. was a member of the United Mine Workers when in Alabama. Upon moving North he joined the longshoremen's union. His experience in the local was unsatisfactory because the union had little or no power, and the competition of unorganized immigrant groups was too great.

18—As an organized garment worker in S—, M. J. has had no difficulty in getting work. He claims to have received the same consideration as other workers. When working he receives $60.00 a week.

19—A. T. F. is a tailor and presser and belongs to the Cleaners and Dyers Union. Before coming affiliated with the union the cleaners gave much trouble. As a member he gets better prices and more satisfactory work.

[171]

20—After several attempts E. P., a linotypist was admitted to the local typographical union in ———. There are benefits to be derived from labor unions but "not so long as efforts are made to retard the Negro, especially the efficient ones." He is able to get only temporary work because the better shops claim that employment is given on a seniority basis.

21—Nine years ago C. W. started his efforts to join the Electrical Workers Union in ———. In December, 1928, he was given a card granting him permission to work as a union man on six months probation. While attempting to join the union he was pulled off four jobs. In the face of this situation he believes that "any collective or combined efforts are worth joining because of the benefits which can be derived. On the other hand, unions can be harmful to you because of their propaganda—and "their malicious acts such as bombings."

22—A. H. is a hod carrier and a member of the union. Despite the national attitude of the hod carriers union, he complains against the local attitude for several reasons. Among them are the following: (1) the initiation fee is too high, (2) Negroes are discriminated against, (3) Italian foremen sometimes replace Negroes with Italians, (4) often have to pay to remain on job.

23—C. F., a carpenter, belongs to the union of his craft. He receives sick benefits as well as higher wages. Because some foremen to try to keep Negroes off jobs, hiring whites in their places and because the union makes no special efforts to secure work for Negroes, he feels that he is not getting all of the advantages.

24—Membership in the Marine Cooks and Stewards Union has meant regular employment and good pay to J. A.

25—I. F. is a plasterer, who for two years tried to join the plasterers union only to be told that the books were closed. Since becoming a member he has found the protection, wages and hours sponsored by the union to be to his advantage.

26—J. W. T. joined the Federal employees union in ———, and has received all the courtesies and privileges of membership. Recently he was elected delegate from this union to the Trades and Labor Assembly.

27—G. S. M. is a post office employee in ———. Upon coming North from Texas he was employed as a strikebreaker in a packing house. Because of threats he quit, and entered the

Postal Service Motor Vehicle Service Department. At the beginning everything possible was done by the foremen and the white employees to retard his progress. After a time he was allowed to learn painting—and became a mail truck painter. Despite the fact that he belongs to the union of U. S. Motor Vehicle Employees and was elected a trustee for three years he believes that "considering all things locally the unions are no good for the colored man."

28—C. W. is a miner working one day a week. He belongs to the United Mine Workers Union. To him the union's "purpose is good but its functioning is awful." Prejudice and segregation make membership troublesome.

29—E. P. belongs to the Musicians Protective Association in an Illinois city and has experienced many inconveniences because of that membership. He "could suggest some improvements in unions which would be of advantage to the Negro musician but which the union would not tolerate."

30—W. M. Jr., has been a brickyard worker for two years. Because of the accident and death benefit features of membership in the United Brick and Clay Workers he has found his membership in that organization quite valuable.

31—H. L. has had very good success as a union molder in two mid-western cities. His affiliation with the International Molders Union in a white local has been a happy one. So happy has it been that he can see no "manner in which the union might harm one."

32—J. W. as worked as a miner for fifteen years and later became an auto mechanic. He has helped to set up union and because of the way "unions are conducted now, to my mind, they are more of a bar than help to a colored man."

33—J. L. M. believes that any trade organization can get better working conditions and wages than a non-organized trade. He is a stationary engineer and was formerly secretary of his local which was composed of white and colored members.

34—M. J. is a chipper. For two years he belonged to the building trades union, but was unable to get regular work. His complaint is that Negro members must pay the regular fees and get less work.

35—H. W. is a baker and belongs to the bakers union. It is opinion that the "unions themselves are alright but sometimes the members do not keep the oath they take."

36—L. was readily accepted as a member of the bricklayers union ten years ago. He has found, however, that the locals are not racially fair. He has been discriminated against in getting work and the business agents have not "played fair." The unions are willing for Negroes to join, but seemingly do everything possible to prevent their going on a job until absolutely necessary. In seasons of slack work there is scarcely a chance.

NON-UNION WORKERS

37—C. O. is at present employed as an automobile mechanic though he is a mechanical engineer by trade. He attempted to join the union of his craft in ——, but was refused, being told that he must have experience in an organized shop. He could not get that experience unless he had a union card.

38—H. W. is a plumber, a master plumber, in ——. He took the examination to join the Journeymen Plumbers Union, is reported to have passed, later reported as failing. He was also informed that he was rejected because two plumbers would not vouch for him. His jobs have been bombed several times, making it difficult to secure contracts. H. H. feels that unions have done him irreparable harm.

39—C. S. was a non-union carpenter in the South but tried to join the carpenters union in —— when he moved there in 1921. Oddly enough the business agent advised him not to join because the fees were too much for a Negro to pay, and it would be too difficult for him to secure work.

40—R. J. is a decorator and paper hanger in C—. While working on one job in an apartment house, the business agent of the janitors union threatened to have him taken off unless he joined the painters union. He tried but he did not have the fee at the time, and since then they have kept him waiting.

41—J. D. is a plasterer who tried to join the plasterers union in ——, but was told he would have to join the hod carriers union as no "niggers" were permitted to work as plasterers in the building trade of that city.

42—A. J. is unemployed at present, though a painter by trade. Fifty dollars kept him from joining the painters union in ——. This was not the initiation fee, but the amount supposedly demanded by the agent who would secure a membership for him.

43—A. T. is a machinist and has a white helper. Some helpers have protested but the foreman has told them to work or get out. The machinists union will not admit him. At one time he was president of a miscellaneous local composed entirely of Negro workers.

44—W. W. is a carpenter and contractor. He is not in the union because colored members cannot join with white locals in this southern city, and there are not enough Negro carpenters to establish a local of their own.

45—W. E. V. is a common laborer and has not joined the union because he has seen too many cases where they will not allow colored men the same chances as whites.

46—G. H. A. is now a building contractor. Prior to becoming a contractor he has been a brick mason, carpenter and stationary engineer, and had belonged to the union of each craft. While admitting that unions have considerably improved the living conditions of the workers he states that the Negro worker suffers because he is kept from working on the best jobs.

47—J. A. J. is an experienced millwright. Because of color he was unable to secure work on coming to ——. Now he believes that unions "will not give a colored man a square deal. When he is in the union he has to do what the union says, and can work only when sent out on a job."

48—G. C. is a steam engineer and has had only two jobs in his life. He has not joined the local union in —— because he has not needed to do so, and it costs $25.00.

49—W. J. is a decorator and has not been concerned with unions because from the experience of others it seemed impossible to get sufficient work to keep employed.

50—As a blacksmith S. B. always found the best jobs and many times the only jobs for colored men in open shops. He realizes that unions are powerful, but in his case they are too powerful. He has always had to work under the union scale.

NEGRO MEMBERSHIP IN AMERICAN LABOR UNIONS

INDEX